A Practical Guide for Magnetic and Spiritual Healing

A Practical Guide for Magnetic and Spiritual Healing

Jussara Korngold

Copyright © 2017
UNITED STATES SPIRITIST COUNCIL Jussara Korngold
First Edition 2017

All rights reserved. No part of this publication may be reproduced, stored in or introduced into a retrieval system, or transmitted, in any form, or by any means (electronic, mechanical, photocopying, recording or otherwise) without the prior written permission of the publisher, except in the case of brief quotations and if the source and publisher are mentioned.

Main entry under title:
A Practical Guide for Magnetic and Spiritual Healing

ISBN-13: 9781948109024
ISBN-10: 1948109026

LCCN: 2017916088
United States Spiritist Council

Contact: info@spiritist.us
www.spiritist.us

Cover design: Mauro de Souza Rodrigues
Chakras Drawings: Claudia Stranings Jennings

Library of Congress Cataloging-in-Publication Data
– A Practical Guide for Magnetic and Spiritual Healing/Jussara Korngold

1. Religious Philosophy 2. Spiritist Doctrine 3. Christianity

Manufactured in the United States of America

Table of Contents

Foreword · ix
Introductory Messages · xi
Passes · xi
Laying on of Hands ·xii

Chapter 1　The Act of Healing throughout History · · · · · · · · · 1
Chapter 2　Passes Pivotal Points (PPP)· 7
Chapter 3　The Spiritist Approach to The Pass · · · · · · · · · · · · 10
Chapter 4　Fluids · 12
　　　　　　4.1 Universal Cosmic Fluid (UCF) · · · · · · · · · · · 12
　　　　　　4.2 Vital Fluid · 15
　　　　　　4.3 Spirit, Perispirit and the Physical Body · · · · · · 19
　　　　　　4.4 The Aura · 21
　　　　　　4.5 Centers of Force or Vital Centers · · · · · · · · · · 22
　　　　　　The Streams of Vitality · 27
　　　　　　Crown or Coronal Center · · · · · · · · · · · · · · · · · · 28
　　　　　　Frontal or Brow Center· 32
　　　　　　Laryngeal or Throat Center· · · · · · · · · · · · · · · · · 35
　　　　　　Cardiac or Heart Center· 37
　　　　　　Gastric or Umbilical Center · · · · · · · · · · · · · · · · · 39

	Splenic or Spleen Center	41
	Genesic or Root Center	43
Chapter 5	The Three Types of Passes	45
	The Process of Passes	47
	Psychical Force, Fluids and Magnetism	48
Chapter 6	The Pass Giver	52
	Recommendations to The Pass Giver	54
Chapter 7	The Patient	56
Chapter 8	When the Pass is Helpful	59
Chapter 9	When Passes Are Not Convenient	61
Chapter 10	Where Passes May Be Performed	63
Chapter 11	Practical Guidance	69
Chapter 12	Absentee Pass	71
Chapter 13	The Pass Outside Of The Spiritist Center	73
Chapter 14	The Service Of "Spiritual Passes"	78
Chapter 15	The Healing Mediums	87
Chapter 16	Magnetic Properties of Matter	90
	Modification of the Properties of Matter	90
	16.1 Magnetic Curative Action	90
	16.2 Magnetized Water	91
Chapter 17	Types of Passes	94
	17.1 Laying on of Hands	94
	Examples Of Laying On Of Hands	97
	17.2 Longitudinal Passes	97
	The Five Movements Of Longitudinal Pass	100
	17.3 Rotational Passes	101
	17.4 Transverse Passes	102
	17.5 Perpendicular Passes	103
Chapter 18	The Healing Breath	104
	18.1 The Cold Healing Breath or Cold Insufflations	105

18.2 The Hot Healing Breath or Hot
Insufflations ···106
18.3 The Healing Breath ··················108

Bibliography ······························113

Foreword

THE NATURE OF THIS PRACTICAL guide requires an explanation.

In our earnest desire to promote Spiritism further in the United States, we realize the tremendous need for material in the English language. Only through instructive books and comprehensible brochures will we, undoubtedly, be able to spread the principles of Spiritism and create and form new groups of knowledgeable practitioners.

Since we departed Brazil in 1993, our efforts have been directed toward this goal.

While compiling and translating most of its contents in order to formulate them into book form, we have attempted to satisfy the great need for this type of material in English. We sincerely hope that it can be of assistance and benefit to other groups, who sincerely dedicate themselves to the blessed task passes.

May God's blessings be with you,

Jussara Korngold
New York, 2017

Introductory Messages

Passes[1]

And he pleaded earnestly with him: "My daughter is dying; please, come and lay your hands on her so that she will be healed and live." (Mk 5:23)

JESUS USED TO LAY HIS hands on the unwell, transmitting the benefits of health to them. Due to his loving power, he knew about the smallest imbalances of nature and possessed the means needed to restore harmony to it.

More action of the Divine Master was without meaning. Aware of this truth, the apostles began the laying on of fraternal hands in the name of the Lord, becoming instruments of Divine Mercy.

Today, in revived Christianity, there is once again help from the invisible world through the laying on of hands. Passes are transfusions of psychic powers, by which precious spiritual energies emanate from the messengers of Christ to both donor and

---

1 Pass -- "A moving of the hands over or along something."
Webster's New Collegiate Dictionary
Pass: to serve as a medium of exchange. Merriam-Webster's Collegiate Dictionary

beneficiary. They represent the continuance of the Master's efforts to alleviate suffering in the world.

Of course it would be audacious for modern disciples to expect results as sublime as those obtained by Jesus when he healed paralytics, mentally disturbed individuals and agonizing people. The Master knew, whereas we are learning to know.

Nevertheless, we cannot disregard his lessons. We must continue his work of love by means of fraternal hands.

Jesus' providential service may be extended to wherever there is a sincere mental attitude for doing good.

How the good is done does not matter; what does matter is recognizing the fact that it can and should be done in his name.

Emmanuel / Francisco C. Xavier
The Way, the Truth and the Life – Item 153 – Edicei 2012

Laying on of Hands

In the book Spiritist Opinion,[2] written by the spirit André Luiz, through the mediumship of Francisco C. Xavier, we can read that, "the act of laying on of hands is not just for a transfusion of psychic energies. It is the ideal tool to balance the mind, and an effective aid to all kinds of treatments. Discouragement and sadness, as much as dissatisfaction and revolt, are syndromes of the soul; they establish imbalances and promote diseases in the body. Where there is health, these states of mind bring about organic disasters; when there is disease, they are equivalent to predispositions for premature death; but this is not all. In every mental

---

2 *Opinião Espírita*, not yet translated into English

unbalance, negative forces enter more easily into action, starting obsessive processes of unpredictable duration. If we use antibiotics as a substance to frustrate the development of microorganisms in the physical body, why not adopt passes as an agent capable of impeding depressive hallucinations of the soul?

If we tend to asepsis, in relation to the body, why neglect, asepsis in the spirit? The application of healing forces in magnetism is present in the fluid-therapy with the same importance as the use of providential emanations from electricity. Spirits and mediums help us cultivate passes, by means of prayer, and with the respect that is due to one of the most legitimate complements to ordinary therapy.

Certainly, abuses of hypnosis are responsible for the regrettable flightiness in showroom treacheries, all done in the name of science. These are new disturbances in the world; however, passes and the dignity of prayer have always been a Divine aid to human needs. It is enough to remember the Gospel, which depicts Jesus by the sufferers' side, imposing his hands."

CHAPTER 1

The Act of Healing throughout History

ACCORDING TO FOWLER'S CONCISE ENGLISH Dictionary to heal is "to restore to health," and health is defined as "soundness of body." The definition found in the Oxford Dictionary is very similar "(cause to) become healthy and sound; restore a (person) to health, cure." Definitions of health can vary, however, and are influenced by the emphasis of one aspect or another and by the sociological approach. For example, the World Health Organization defines health as a state of complete physical, mental and social well being, while the medical profession's definition of health emphasizes the absence of disease or biological disturbances.

There are many branches on the healing tree. Today, there is a division between orthodox medicine and spiritual healing. However, the gaps between them are slowly closing. Doctors, nurses, therapists, and psychologists are healers, but because of the mentioned division the word, "Healer" is usually associated with a Spiritual Healer.

The power of healing through one's gaze, touch, and the laying on of hands is also one of the forms by which spiritual action is exerted over the world. God, the source of all life, is the principle of physical health, as it is of moral perfection and supreme beauty. Some individuals, by prayer and magnetic élan, attract this influx to themselves, this radiance of the divine force, which drives off the impure fluids that cause suffering. The spirit of charity, devotion verging on sacrifice, and of forgetfulness of self, is the condition necessary to acquire and preserve this power, one of the most wonderful ones bestowed by God on humans.

This power, this superiority of the mind over matter, has asserted itself in all ages.

Let us look at some of the different aspects of passes throughout history and the world. In Egypt there were healing priests called "Shrine Bearers" who were very advanced, and learned their medical arts from six books which formed part of a total of 42 works, brought to Egypt by a different race of people before the flood. Their six books dealt with: The Constitution of the Body, Diseases, Instruments, Drugs, Eyes, and The Maladies of Women.

There were also many Gods of healing: Thoth, Imhotep, and others. Thoth, or Tehuti, was a principal god of healing. He was also associated with time and karma. Another Egyptian healing god was the Cat Goddess, Bastet, who protected the mentally sick. Isis, mistress of magic, was invoked for her nurturing qualities and healing energies. Horus, son of Isis, favored healing young children and physical wounds. Anubis, patron of anesthetics, was believed to watch over the spirit while it was separated from the body during surgery.

In China pass givers were more medically trained and practiced acupuncture. The goal was to prevent diseases and it was said, "when one became ill one would stop paying the doctors." The Chinese had a concept of a "subtle body" or what might also be called "Perispirit." The Goddess Kuan Yin was believed to cure all illnesses.

Healing in ancient India was quite advanced in the treatment of diseases. Records show that they were efficient with performing surgery, brain and cesarean operations, as well as herbal treatments for all sorts of complaints. Healing was also based on the importance of mind and body.

The inhabitants of Greece and Rome, as well as other populations of the Mediterranean, had strong healing traditions. Socrates knew the importance of healing the soul in order to heal the body. Medicine as it is known today ultimately originated in Greece with the rational school.

It is important to note that the Hebrews and the Essenes also based their healing on the cure of the soul as well as the body. Like the Egyptians, their pass givers were initiated and once they became elders they could cast out the "devil" from people. They worked with the "etheric body" and believed that it should be adjusted before physical healing could take place.

Vespasian, by the laying on of hands, cured a partially blind man and another with a paralyzed hand.[3] The cures obtained by Apollonius of Tyana are no less celebrated.

However, the greatest healer that has ever existed on Earth was Jesus Christ. The primitive Christians witnessed many healing events leading to a strong tradition of the "laying on of hands". This practice continues today, although in a modified way.

Some ancient practices advocated the need for a cure of the subtle body before any permanent physical cure could be achieved. We also notice this in the Spiritist approach to healing. To heal, human beings must be considered in their wholeness – body plus spirit.

Despite modern medicine's incredible technological advances, its main focus is the physical body. This eliminates the opportunity to see both sides – physical *and* spiritual. Equilibrium is

---

3 Tacitus, *The Histories*, Book IV, ch. LXXXI.

needed for perfect health and is frequently lost. When this occurs, there is little or no harmony between body and soul.

All the healers of antiquity were initiates and priests. In modern medicine there is a great demand for highly specialized training, and this leads us to ask, "Who can heal?" When considering spiritual healing through passes, we can safely say that everyone is able to heal to some degree, and we will be exploring this concept throughout this work.

In the 18th century, Dr. F. Anton Mesmer gave an important contribution to the field of healing, carrying out his research into animal magnetism and its properties. Also known as mesmerism, magnetic passes developed into hypnotherapy and still survives today.

In his book, *Into the Unseen*[4], Leon Denis says. *"In modern times, circa the 1830s, a holy Bavarian priest, the Prince Alexander of Hohenlohe, possessed this admirable faculty. He always proceeded by praying and invocation to God, and the fame of his cures resounded throughout Europe. He healed the blind, the deaf, and the dumb; a crowd of sick and infirm persons, constantly renewed, besieged his dwelling house.*

In France, other thaumaturgists attracted crowds of people full of sorrow and despair. Cahagnet, Puységur, du Potet, Deleuze and their disciples did prodigies. Even today, many healers, more or less profitably, take care of themselves with the help of the spirits.[5]

These simple people, these believers, are puzzles and embarrassing points for official medical science, so impotent in the face of pain, notwithstanding its proud pretensions. Charcot, a subtle observer, at the end of

---

4 Published by USSF – 2017, translated by HMM.
5 The author clearly used the term thaumaturge or thaumaturgist to refer to certain healing mediums and magnetizers who only cured those who could afford them.

his life recognized their power. He wrote, in an English journal, a study which have become famous, Faith-Healing. Indeed, faith, which is itself a source of life, can suffice to restore health. The facts demonstrate it with irresistible eloquence. In the most diverse circles, good men: the cure of Ars, Mr. Vigne, a Protestant of the Cévennes, Russian Orthodox Father John of Kronstadt; others still, both in the Catholic sanctuaries, as well as in those of Islam or India, have obtained innumerable cures by prayer.

This has proved it: above all human churches and detached from all rites, sects, and formulas, there is a supreme focus which the soul can attain through the impetus of faith, which draws from forces, assistance, and lights that cannot be appreciated or understood by those who ignore God and do not want to pray. In reality, magnetic healing requires neither passes nor special formulas, but only the ardent desire to relieve others, the sincere and profound calling of the soul to God, the source and principle of all forces."

Many people confuse a magnetic pass with a spiritual pass, so it is useful to clarify that when the pass is magnetic, the transfusion is of the pass giver's own fluids to the patient; in spiritual pass, the transmission is mainly of spiritual fluids, through the pass giver, who acts as the channel. When the pass is spiritual, the pass giver does not become depleted of energies, where as that may be the case in magnetic passes. A magnetizer who is well intentioned, however, inevitably receives help from the Spirits during their work, whether they ask for it or not. In this case their own potential will be greatly enhanced (see item 2.5 – The Three Types of Passes).

It is clear that all people have a common healing inheritance, differentiated solely by tradition and custom. From the Egyptians, Hindus, Chinese, Celts and Druids, to the American Indians and Australian Aborigines, healing is indeed a need that surpasses all national boundaries and can be found in the very essence of human nature.

From these considerations one fact emerges: that, perpetually, in all ages, the invisible world has collaborated with the world of the living, showering upon its inspirations, coming to our aid. The miracles of the past are the phenomena of the present; names alone change while spiritual facts are eternal.

CHAPTER 2

Passes Pivotal Points (PPP)

WE HAVE LISTED BELOW THE pivotal points for those who intend to dedicate themselves to the services of passes.

1. To comprehend, master, and exercise adequate techniques in the transmission of fluids, based on simplicity, discretion and Christian ethics are essential.
2. To correctly associate the need for concentration, prayer and irradiation with the pass process allowing you to feel the transfusion of vital fluidic energies during the pass, thus making the transmission easier.
3. To understand the necessity of a special ambient combined with special conditions for the atmosphere of that ambient, as well as a favorable situation for the application of the pass.
4. To rigorously observe moral, physical and spiritual necessities, combined with knowledge of the doctrine in order to be able to perform the act of giving pass with efficiency and seriousness at all times.
5. To observe simplicity and the correct form in which to apply the pass, avoiding rituals, strange attitudes and gestures. These gestures incorrectly applied lead to

conditioning on the part of the pass giver and misinterpretation on the part of the patient.
6. To illustrate the correct form of the application of the pass through demonstrations, which can be observed by an entire group of participants.
7. To recognize the need for and to exercise constant discipline during the pass without any ostensive display of mediumistic manifestation. Avoid counseling the patient during the pass, as well as being conscious of the fact that each application should be given in silence.
8. To recognize that physical contact during the pass is improper. Contact may cause a negative reaction and be an embarrassment to the patient. It is totally unnecessary within the ethics and simplicity of the doctrine, since all fluid energy transmitted from the pass giver to the patient is by means of the aura and not by means of the epidermis. This has been proven through the use of the Kirlian photography, which clearly show the flow of energy from the pass giver to the patient without physical contact.
9. To develop initiative with discipline and discretion in the task of helping members of the group during their mediumistic development by means of spiritual passes, as well as, those who may be suffering a temporary imbalance due to either a pathological or obsessive cause.
10. To be aware that during the pass the medium should not rely solely on good faith, but rather should learn to depend on oneself and one's own efficiency.
11. To understand the necessity of working with a minimum of three pass givers (as a team and not individually), in order to achieve and sustain the concentrated vibrations required. Every Spiritist Group or Center, should maintain

regular Sessions of Passes. They should not be carried out at home except when following a "Gospel at Home" meeting, or in the case of an emergency due to physical illness. In the last case it is important to remember the absolute necessity for the team to prepare the ambient before commencing the passes through prayer and specified reading (e.g.: The Gospel According to Spiritism, or other instructive and uplifted spiritual message).

12. To know in which situation the pass would be beneficial, harmful or of no effect. Every Spiritist Center or Group should offer passes along with Gospel and doctrinal instruction, and inform the general public as to its collaboration with the pass giver in order to receive full benefit from the pass. Passes should always be administered in a room designated solely as the Pass Sanctuary.

CHAPTER 3

The Spiritist Approach to The Pass

THE SPIRITIST DEFINITION OF HEALTH is characterized by the degree of a Spirit's commitment to the natural laws. In the words of the Spirit Emmanuel "...health means the perfect harmony of the soul. In order to finally obtain this, however, it is often necessary to receive valuable contributions in the form of illnesses and deficiencies pertaining to Earth." (*The Consoler* – question 95)

Nevertheless, as the human being consists in one's essence of soul, perispirit and physical body; it is important to preserve the good functioning of the latter, not forgetting that the quality of our thoughts affects our perispirit, which accordingly reacts on our physical body. A Protecting Spirit stated his concern by saying: "So then, love your soul and also look after your body, which is the instrument of your soul." (*The Gospel According to Spiritism* – Chapter 7 – Paragraph 11)

Spiritism tells us that following the teachings of Jesus is a secure pathway towards spiritual evolution and eventual purification. "Love being the finest sentiment that exists, summarizes the complete doctrine of Jesus." (*The Gospel According to Spiritism* – Chapter 11 – Paragraph 8)

Jesus taught us to love our neighbor and the pass is one of the many ways we can practice this. In Spiritist Centers it is traditional to hold meetings in which passes are offered. There we can observe three aspects of the pass:

- It offers the patient some relief from suffering, even though a cure might not necessarily be achieved.
- It offers the pass giver an opportunity to be charitable and to serve one's neighbor.
- It offers the spiritual workers a more effective means of helping those in need.

Passes, as practiced in Spiritist Centers, can be described as a transmission of fluids coming directly from the spiritual world. These fluids are manipulated by the Spiritual Benefactors and channeled through incarnate pass givers, who donate a portion of their own "vital fluid" to assist the patient.

Great pass givers, who were also magnetizers, could achieve instant cure for many ailments. But in Spiritism we trust the Spiritual Benefactors to give the patient that which he or she needs most. This takes into account the Law of Action and Reaction and the fact that many difficult situations, and even certain illnesses, are exactly what our souls need. We cannot escape the Universal Law and the truth is that we are accountable for all our actions past, present and future.

"Heal the sick, cleanse the lepers, raise the dead, cast out devils, freely ye have received, freely give." (Matthew 10:8). It is also expected from spiritists that no charge be made for the pass, whether offered inside or outside of a Spiritist Center.

CHAPTER 4

Fluids

4.1 Universal Cosmic Fluid (UCF)[6]

The universal fluid is elementary primitive matter, of which the modifications and transformations constitute the innumerable varieties of the bodies of nature. As far as the elementary universal principle is concerned, it offers two distinct states; that of etherealization, or imponderability, that one can consider as the primitive, normal state, and that of materialization, or ponderability, which is in some ways only consecutive. The intermediary point is that of the transformation of the fluid into tangible matter; but there is no sudden transition, for one can consider our imponderable fluids as a boundary between the two states.

Each one of these two states provides a place necessary to special phenomena. To the second belong those of the visible world, and to the first those of the invisible one. Those called *material phenomena* are, properly speaking, in the domain of science. The solution of the others are designated *spiritual or physic phenomena*, because they are allied more especially to the existence of spirits,

---

6 An excerpt from the *"Genesis"* – Allan Kardec – Chapter 14, Items 2 to 6, published by SAB 2003.

and are among the prerogatives of Spiritism. But, as spiritual and material lives are in a continual contact, the phenomena of these two orders are presented often simultaneously. The human being, in a state of incarnation, can only have the perception of the physical phenomena, which are connected with the material life. Those that belong to the exclusive domain of spiritual life escape the eye of the material senses, and can be perceived only in the spiritual state.[7]

In an etherealized state, the universal fluid is not uniform. Without ceasing to be ethereal, it is submitted to modifications varied in their kind and more numerous than in a state of tangible matter. These modifications constitute distinct fluids, which, although proceeding from the same principle, are endowed with special properties, and give place to particular phenomena of the invisible world.

All being relative, these fluids have for the spirits, who are themselves fluidic, an appearance as material similar to that of the objects for the incarnated, and are for them that which the substances of the terrestrial world are for us. They elaborate and combine them, in order to produce determined effects, as people do with their materials, yet by different processes.

But there, as it is here, is only given to the most enlightened spirits to comprehend the *role* of the constitutive elements of their world. The ignorant people of the invisible world are as incapable of explaining the phenomena of which they are witnesses, and in which they cooperate often mechanically, as the ignorant of earth

---

[7] The name *psychical* phenomena expresses the idea better than spiritual does, as these phenomena rest upon the properties and attributes of the soul, or rather on the perispiritual fluids, which are inseparable from the soul. This qualification attaches them more intimately to the order of natural facts, regulated by laws. One can then admit them as psychical effects without allowing them the title of miracles.

are of explaining the effects of light or of electricity, or of explaining the process of seeing and hearing.

The fluidic elements of the spiritual world elude our instruments of analysis, and the perception of our senses. They are things suited to tangible, and not to ethereal, matter. Spiritual substances belong to a midst so different from ours that we can judge them only by comparisons as imperfect as those by which a person born blind seeks to form an idea of the theory of color.

But among these fluids a few are intimately joined to corporeal life, and belong to the terrestrial universe. In default of direct perception of cause, one can observe the effects of them, and acquire some knowledge of their nature with precision. This study is essential for it is the key limited to a multitude of phenomena, which are inexplicable by the laws of matter alone.

The starting-point of the universal fluid is the degree of absolute ethereality, of which nothing can give us an idea. Its opposite point is its transformation into material substance. Between these two extremes exist innumerable transformations, which are allied more or less to one another. The fluids, which are the nearest materiality (consequently the least pure), are composed of what might be called the *spiritual terrestrial atmosphere.* In this midst widely different degrees of ethereality whence the incarnated and disincarnated inhabitants of the earth are found and draw the necessary elements for the economy of their existence. These fluids, however subtle and impalpable they may be to us, are nevertheless of comparatively gross nature to the ethereal fluids of the superior regions.

It is the same on the surface of all worlds, saving the differences of constitution and vitality proper to each. The less material life there is, the less the spiritual fluids have of affinity with matter.

The name *"spiritual fluid"* is not as accurate as it is really always more or less refined. There is nothing really spiritual, but the soul or intelligent principle. We designate fluids thus by comparison, and chiefly by reason of their affinity with spirits. They constitute the substance of the spiritual world. That is why they are called spiritual fluids.

Who understands the intricate constitution of tangible matter? It is, perhaps, compact only in relation to our senses; and that which seems to prove this is the easiness with which it is traversed by spiritual fluids, and the spirits to whom it is no more of an obstacle than are transparent bodies to light.

Tangible matter, having for a primitive element the ethereal cosmic fluid, must be able, *by becoming disintegrated*, to return to a state of etherealization, as the diamond, the hardest of bodies, can be volatized into impalpable gas. *The solidification of matter is in reality only a transitory state of the universal fluid, which can return to its primitive state when the conditions of cohesion cease to exist.* Who knows if, in a tangible state, matter is not susceptible of acquiring a sort of etherealization which would give to it peculiar properties? Certain phenomena, which appear authentic, lean towards such a supposition as this. We do not yet posses all the beacon-lights of the invisible world; and the future has in reserve for us, without doubt, the knowledge of new laws, which will allow us to comprehend that which is still a mystery to us.

4.2 Vital Fluid

In *The Spirits' Book*[8] the term vital principle is used to define the material and organic life that is common to all living beings regardless of its source, from plants to humankind. As life can exist when

---

8 Allan Kardec - Part II – Introduction – USSF 2017

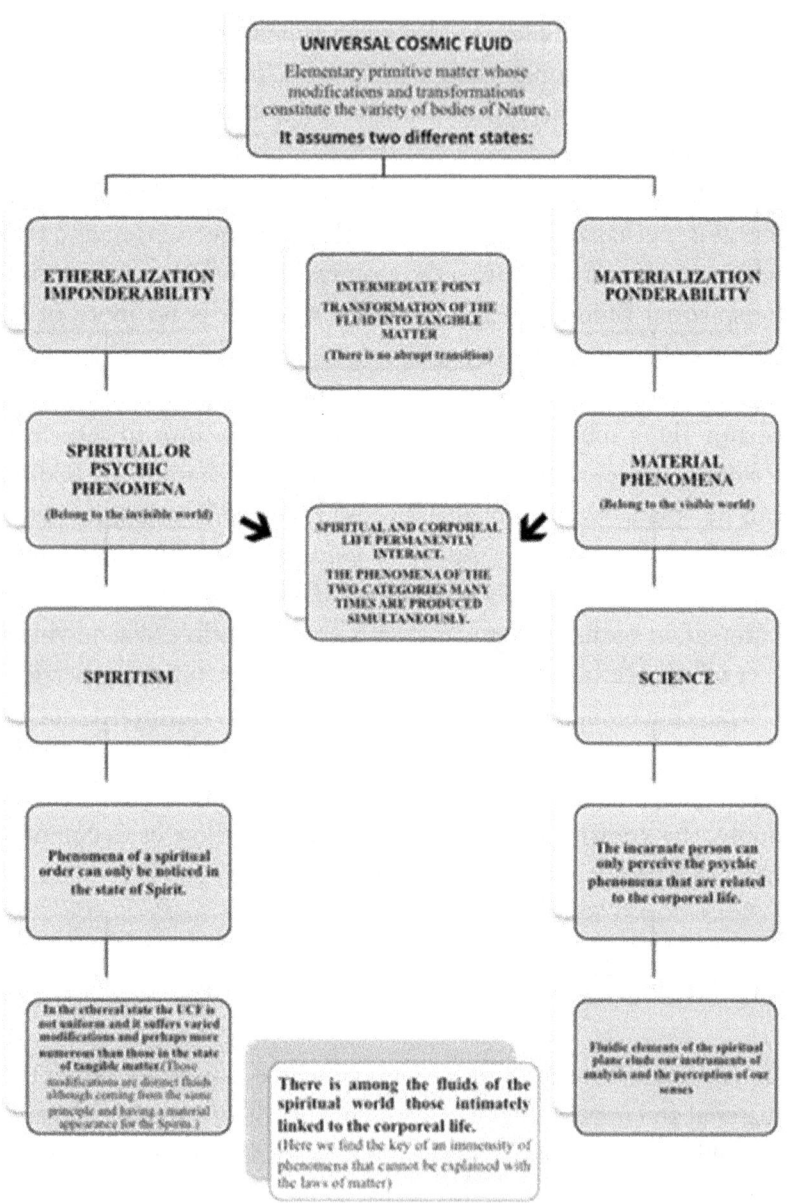

a being does not have the ability to think, the vital principle is a distinct and independent element.

Vital Fluid is a modification of the Universal Fluid. It generates nervous impulses that circulate through the body via the nervous system.

In *The Spirits' Book* we find excellent instructions from the spirits when replying to Kardec's questions, regarding vital fluid:

60. **Does the same force unite the elements of matter in organic and inorganic bodies?**
    "Yes, the same law of attraction exists for all."
61. **Is there any difference between the matter of organic and inorganic bodies?**
    "It is the same. The only difference is that in organic bodies it is animalized."
62. **What is the cause of the animalization of matter?**
    "The union of matter with the vital principle."
63. **Is the vital principle present in a specific agent, or is it a property of organized matter? Simply put, is it an effect or a cause?**
    "It is both. Life is an effect produced by an agent acting on matter. Without matter, this agent is not life, just as matter cannot be alive without this agent. It gives life to every being that absorbs it."
64. **Spirit and matter are two essential elements of the universe. Is the vital principle a third?**
    "There is no question that it is necessary for the makeup of the universe, but its source is a special variation of universal matter. For you, it is an element like oxygen or hydrogen, which are not primordial elements because everything derives from the same foundation."

65. Does the vital principle reside in any bodies that we know?
"Its source is the universal fluid, which is what you call the magnetic or electric fluid, only animalized. It is an intermediary, the link between the spirit and matter."

66. Is the vital principle the same for all organic beings?
"Yes, but adapted according to each species. This principle gives organic beings the power of initiating movement and activity. They are distinguished from inert matter by their ability to produce spontaneous movement. Inert matter can be moved, but it does not initiate movement."

The quality and quantity of the Vital Fluid will vary according to the nature of the living beings. Once it is weakened, it can be restored through the absorption and assimilation of substances in which it can be found (respiratory system, skin, and food.) The first state pertains to the invisible world, which is qualified as spiritual or psychic phenomena, and thus belongs to the field of Spiritism.

The quantity of vital fluid present in all organic beings is not the same. It varies in the different species of living beings, and is not always the same in the same individual or individuals who have very small quantities. Consequently, certain species have a more active and persistent life due to the abundance of vital fluid present in their bodies.

The vital fluid contained in a given organism may be exhausted, and become insufficient to support life, unless it is renewed by the absorption of substances that contain it.

The vital fluid may be transferred from one individual to another. For those who possess copious amounts, it may be given to someone else who is deficient. In certain cases, this may rekindle the vital flame when on the verge of being snuffed out.[9]

---

9 KARDEC, Allan – The Spirits' Book – Book 1, Chapter 4, Item 70 – USSF 2017

4.3 Spirit, Perispirit and the Physical Body

The word perispirit was first used in a commentary (by Kardec) to the answer given by the spirits to the 93rd question of *The Spirits' Book*. Kardec explains that, *"as a fruit seed is encased within the perisperm, the spirit per se is surrounded by an envelope, which, by comparison, may be called the perispirit."*

According to Allan Kardec's comment following question 135 of *"The Spirits' Book,"* human beings are made up of three essential parts:

1) The body, or material being, similar to animals, and given life by the same vital principle;
2) The soul, or incarnated spirit, which is housed in the body;
3) The intermediary principle, or perispirit, which is a semi-material substance. It is the innermost envelope of the spirit and unites the soul with the body. This three-part nature is equivalent.

Spirits tell us that there are two general elements in the universe: matter and spirit. The spirit is defined as the Intelligent Principle of the Universe, and as Spirits we are the individualization of this principle. Similarly, our bodies are the individualization of the Material Principle.

The perispirit is of a semi-material nature belonging to the realm of matter, although it is a very subtle kind. In fact, the perispirit can be understood as the Spirit's fluidic body. It is one of the most important products of the Universal Cosmic Fluid, being a condensation of this same fluid around a focus of intelligence or soul. Within the composition of the perispirit, the fluid conserves its imponderability and its ethereal qualities. Although it might appear to us as mere vapor, it appears to Spirits as gross matter.

The universe is populated by spirits. During an incarnation, Spirits take on a physical body that is in harmony with the material state of the world in which they live. This physical body is composed of matter, which has been animated by its union with the vital fluid.

Within any one planet, a Spirit draws elements available to form its perispirit. The purity of its elements depends on its degree of moral advancement. In this way we can perceive that the perispirit's inner constitution for each individual is not identical with all other incarnate or discarnate Spirits that populate our planet and the atmosphere around it.

For incarnating, the perispirit is united to the physical body molecule by molecule. This way, the Spirit is enabled to participate in the material world. It can be said that the Spirit wants, the perispirit transmits, and the body executes. Similarly, the body receives external impressions, the perispirit transmits them and the Spirit, being sensitive and intelligent, receives them. So we can see that the spirit and the physical body are acting and interacting with each other by means of a link, which is the perispirit.

Because of its ethereal quality, the perispirit cannot act upon the physical body without the vital fluid, which gives life to the body. This vital fluid, which is a modification of the Universal Fluid, is very similar to an electro-magnetic fluid. This enables it to generate nervous impulses, which circulate in the physical body through the nervous system.

The amount of vital fluid varies according to the species, as well as within the same individual at any given time. Not only does the quantity vary but it can also become exhausted and thus become insufficient to maintain life. It can be renewed by various means such as: absorption and assimilation of substances in which that fluid resides; the respiratory system; through the skin; and the ingestion of foods. It can also be absorbed when transmitted from one individual to another; this is essential in the pass, as we shall see further on.

The perispirit is composed of layers of fluids in different stages of condensation, which allows it to act as mediator between spirit and matter. The layers close to the Spirit are composed of more ethereal fluids whereas those closer to the physical body are more condensed.

The perispirit is formed by the astral body, casual body and vital body:[10]

1) Astral body: the wrapping of the spirit
2) Casual body: the result of the actions lived.
   The Casual Body is one of the components of the fluidic body [perispirit] or spiritual body, described by Lísias in the book Nosso Lar. "We are bearers of dirty clothes to be washed in the tank of human life. This unclean clothes is the casual body, woven by our hands in previous experiences".
3) Vital body: the etheric double or the link between the spirit and matter, responsible for the circulation of the vital fluid or ectoplasm.

4.4 THE AURA

The aura is the energetic emanation of perispiritual fluids that extend beyond the boundaries of the physical organism and is

---

10 Excerpted from the book *A Luz do Eterno Reencontro, - Uma viagem por Nosso Lar*, by Dra. Marlene Nobre, published by FE, 2011

joined by energy extracted from the vital fluid. As humans are constituted of billions of cells, and each cell emits radiation, the total radiation, which is produced, can be described as an "energetic field." This field is continually modified by the Spirit's thoughts and by the conjugation of physio-psychochemical forces, which participate in the formation of the so-called human aura.

Every aura is unique to each individual. It both interpenetrates and surrounds the physical body, presenting colors. The variety of colors depends on the Spirit's level of evolvement. They vary from dark gray to black for Spirits inclined to inferior passions or evil tendencies, or to great brightness for those who have already achieved a higher level of evolvement. Illnesses can be detected from the irregularities in the appearance of the aura because the part of the aura produced by the energies of the physical organism can show lack of functioning. This too affects the coloring. The aura is thought to play an important role in the mechanism of the pass, because the pass process takes place from the pass giver's aura to the patient's aura.

4.5 CENTERS OF FORCE OR VITAL CENTERS[11]

Several studies have shown the existence in the Perispirit of energetic wheels, which controls the currents of energy (from the spirit to matter, and from matter to the spirit) that are ever present as manifestation of life itself. The Spirit Andre Luiz calls them Centers of Force or Vital Centers.

These energetic wheels command with their "extraordinary functions," the various nervous zones and particularly the neural-vegetative

---

11 Also referred to as chakras.

system, inviting through the genes and the genetic codes to a proper and organized work from the neural-endocrines architecture.[12]

It the book *Evolution in Two Worlds*[13] we find the explanation of Andre Luiz of Vital Centers.

The spiritual body or perispirit is the material vehicle of the spirit or discarnate beings that inhabit the extraphysical world. This vehicle is only partially defined by human science, the science of the physical plane, which is also not capable at the moment of recognizing and investigating the presence of the vital centers in the perispirit and their association with specific neural plexuses on the physical body.

Nevertheless, the spiritual body provides all the necessary equipment for the automatic resources that govern billions of microscopic entities that are all in the service of the guiding intelligence behind that spiritual body in the extraphysical realm. Such resources were gradually acquired by the individual essence throughout millennia of efforts and recapitulations in the multiple sectors of its evolution while on the physical plane.

Among the resources and vital points, we identify the crown center, for instance, which is engaged in processes controlling the functional activities of the organs that are described by earthly physiology. Positioned in the central region of the brain (not above the head), the seat of the mind, this vital center assimilates the stimuli from the Superior Plane and thereby guides form, movement, stability, organic metabolism and the consciential life of the

---

12 ANDREA, Jorge – Sexual Forces of the Soul
13 XAVIER, F. C.; VIEIRA, W.; LUIZ, A. (Spirit). Corpo Espiritual [English: The Spiritual Body]. In: Evolução em Dois Mundos [Evolution in Two Worlds]. Federação Espírita Brasileira, Brasília–DF, Brazil, 1st ed., 1959. Chapter II, pp. XXX-XXX. [Translation] PADOVAN, J. C. (translator), 2015 (Translation not in press). [Adapted with permission from the Translator].

incarnate or discarnate being throughout the learning opportunities for which one is responsible while living on a specific planetary abode. Commanded by the spirit, the crown center also supervises the other vital hubs, which follow the impulses in much the same manner that secondary pieces of equipment respond to the injunctions from the master gear in a factory. The first learning experiences are situated therein, from where the coronal center then concatenates and directs all the other vital centers.

Known as secondary hubs due to their dependence on the crown center of energy, the other vital centers are all interwoven by plexiform networks in the psychosoma and, consequently, they are bridged to and relayed onto the physical body as well. Among the secondary centers, the frontal hub is contiguous to the coronal one, and it shows a hierarchically influential predominance over the other secondary centers of energy. The frontal center governs the encephalic cortex and therefore provides a foundation for sensory processing, control of the activity of the endocrine glands and administration of the nervous system in its entire organization, coordination, activity, and mechanism, starting from the sensorial neurons to response mechanism executed by effector cells. The other hierarchically distinguished vital centers include the laryngeal one, which notably controls respiration and phonation; the cardiac center, which directs emotional behavior and the circulation of the elemental forces; the splenic center, which determines all the activities expressed by the blood system within the limitations imposed by the circulatory agent and its corresponding volume; the gastric center, which is responsible for the digestive and absorptive processes of both dense and less dense nutrients that, in one form or another, correspond to the concentrated fluids gaining access to the physical organization; and the genesic center, which guides the modeling of new forms among humans and the establishment of creative stimuli towards work and relationships as well as a sense of fulfillment among the incarnate beings.

In the book *Between Heaven and Earth*[14], instructor Clarencio explains to Andre Luiz and Clarencio that,

> *"Our body of rarefied matter is inwardly governed by seven force centers, which come together in the branches of the plexus. As they vibrate in tune with one another at the inflow of the directive power of the mind, they establish for our use a vehicle of electrical cells, which we may define as an electromagnetic field, in which thoughts vibrates within a closed circuit. Our mental position determines the specific weight of our spirit envelope, and consequently, the 'habitat' it needs. It's only a matter of vibratory pattern. Each of us live within a certain type of wave. The more primitive the condition of the mind, the weaker the vibratory inflow of the thought, inducing the compulsory agglutination of the individual to the regions of embryonic or tormented awareness, where the inferior lives to which it is attuned come together. The increase of the mental flow within the electromagnetic vehicle in which we move after we abandon the earthly body depends on the experience that has been acquired and stored in our own spirit. With this reality in mind, it is easy to understand that we either sublimate or unbalance the delicate agent of our manifestations, according to the type of thought that flows from our inner life. The closer we are to the animal sphere, the greater the obscure condensation of our organization, whereas the more we use our efforts to evolve toward the glorious constructions of the spirit, the greater the subtlety of our envelope, which combines*

---

14 Xavier, Francisco Cândido. Between Heaven and Earth, Edicei 2011, chapter 20, pages 130

easily with beauty, harmony and light that reign in the Divine Creation."

As mentioned in item 2.2, it is in the region where we have a greater condensation of the perispirit that we find the Centers of Force and that the spiritual fluids are absorbed. These spiritual fluids are then transformed into vital fluids when absorbed by the physical body. According to C.W. Leadbeater in the book *"The Chakras"* the word chakra means "wheel" in Sanskrit. The word reflects the Chakras that are a series of vortexes, which look like wheels that exist on the surface of the etheric double of human beings. All these wheels are perpetually rotating, absorbing energy, without which the physical body could not exist. The Chakras or centers of force are points of connection at which energy flows from the vehicle or body of a person to another. When spiritual fluids are absorbed via the perispirit, they circulate among the various centers of force. These are then transformed into vital fluids, which then circulate via the nervous system throughout the whole body. The free flow of fluids in the perispirit, in the centers of force, and in the physical body, can be affected by a series of factors, which can cause physical and psychic imbalances that can then result in illness.

The Centers of force correspond directly with the main human plexus. The seven main ones are as follows:

1. Crown or coronal
2. Frontal or brow
3. Laryngeal or throat
4. Cardiac or heart
5. Gastric or umbilical
6. Spleen or splenic
7. **Genesic or root**

A Practical Guide for Magnetic and Spiritual Healing

The Streams of Vitality

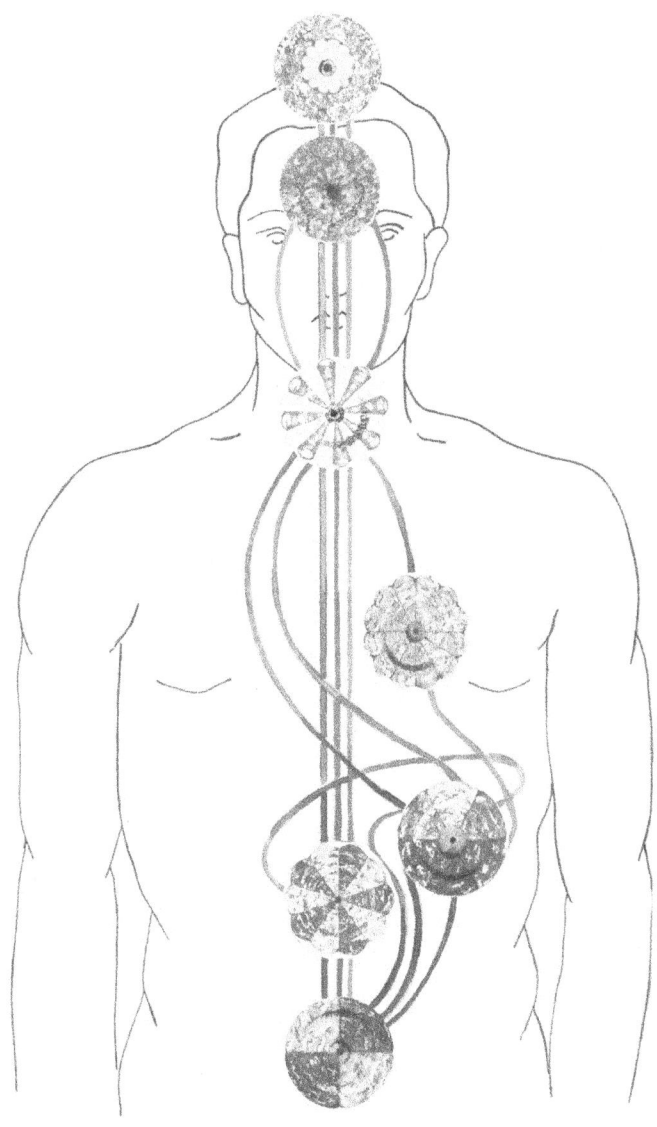

Crown or Coronal Center

Center of Wisdom
GLAND: Pineal gland lies deep within the brain and produces melatonin.
LOCATED: Central region of the brain (top of the head)
RAYS: 960 + 12 – Thousand-Petals Lotus
COLORS: Predominantly Violet (Gold and White)
RESPONSIBILITY: Supervises and commands all the other centers of force and is responsible for the link between the spiritual

and the physical planes. Also related to the development of the brain and spinal system of nerves.

Crown Center: It is located at the central region of the brain, in the direction of the pineal gland. It is not connected with any sympathetic plexus of the physical body. The crown center, however, is associated with the pineal and the pituitary gland. It is the biggest receiver and distributor of spiritual energies. The crown center receives spiritual energies, which are distributed to the other six centers of force, as well as receives energies emanated by those centers of force. In this way the crown center is both a receiver and a donor.

According to instructor Clarencio in the book *Between Heaven and Earth*[15], *as we analyze the physiology of the perispirit, we may classify its force centers by remembering the most important areas of the physical body. Thus, using the best expression for the vehicle that servers us presently, there is the 'crown center', which on earth is considered by Hindu philosophy as being the thousand-petal lotus and the most important center of all due to its high radiation potential and its connection with the mind, the shining seat of the consciousness. The crown center receives first of all, the stimuli of the spirit, commanding the other centers, yet vibrating with them in a perfect system of interdependence. Considering in our exposition the phenomena of the physical body, and satisfying the imperatives of simplicity in our definitions, we can say that the energies of nourishment for the nervous system and its subdivision emanate from this center, and that it is responsible for feeding the thought cells and*

---

15 Xavier, Francisco Cândido. Between Heaven and Earth, Edicei 2011, chapter 20, page 131

for providing all the electromagnetic resources that are indispensable for organic stability. Therefore, it is the great assimilator of the solar energies and rays from the Higher Realms that can favor the sublimation of the soul.

In mediumship it is the center of force that propitiates the affinity, proximity and contact with the Spirits. In magnetism, it perceives and captures the spiritual energy, at the same time that it subtilizes denser energies when transmitted to the spiritual world.

In the book *Evolution in Two Worlds* we find the explanation of Andre Luiz of the Crown Center.[16]

The locus of the interaction between the determinant forces of the spirit and the organized physiopsychosomatic forces, which are effective at the level of the physical body, is to be found primarily in the crown center of energy. Structured with spiritual stimuli, the current of vitalizing energy flows from the crown center, whence it initially has a diffusive action on the constitutive mental matter of the spiritual body, whence it subsequently relays the animated reflexes of our feelings, ideas and actions to all the other centers of the spiritual body. Likewise, these hubs, dependent on one another, later impress similar mental commands upon the organs and other structures of the particular physical constitution, modeling there the agreeable or disagreeable effects of one's influence and conduct.

---

16 XAVIER, F. C.; VIEIRA, W.; LUIZ, A. (Spirit). Corpo Espiritual [English: The Spiritual Body]. In: Evolução em Dois Mundos [Evolution in Two Worlds]. Federação Espírita Brasileira, Brasília–DF, Brazil, 1st ed., 1959. Chapter II, pp. XXX-XXX. [Translation] PADOVAN, J. C. (translator), 2015 (Translation not in press). [Adapted with permission from the Translator].

The mind therefore elaborates constructs that stream from its will by appropriating the elements immediately surrounding it. In this process, the coronal center becomes automatically responsible for fixating the nature of the responsibility related to each one of those constructs. Now thoughts at the spiritual body level, which then brands the sentient being with the happy or unhappy consequences of its conscientious movements in the arena of progress.

Frontal or Brow Center

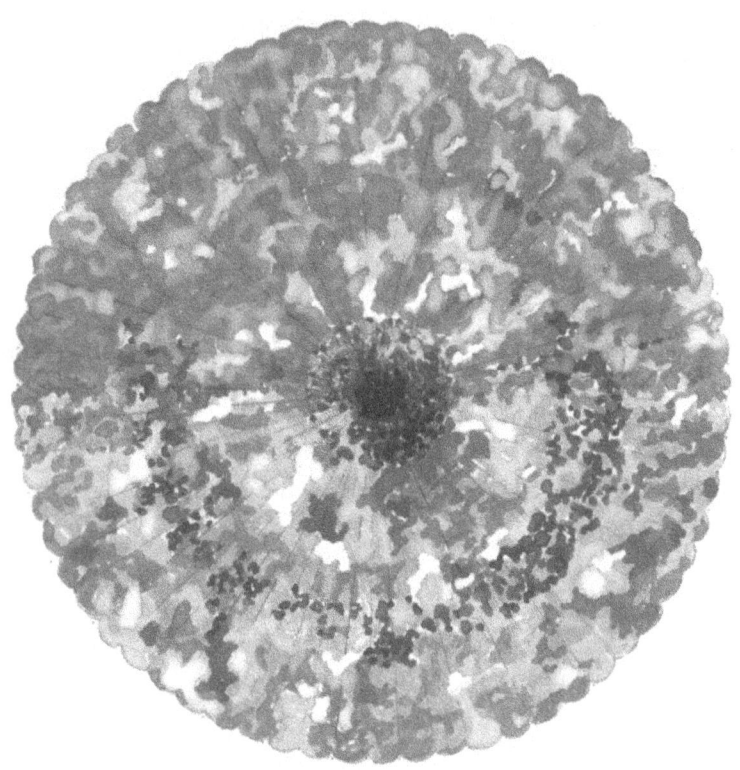

CENTER OF INTUITION
GLAND: Pituitary Gland, which releases hormones influencing body chemistry.
LOCATED: 1st cervical – In the space between the eyebrows
SYMPATHETIC PLEXUS: Carotid
RAYS: 96
COLORS: One half - Rose and Yellow; the other half – Purplish blue

RESPONSIBILITY: The workings of all the superior centers of intelligence and the central nervous system, as well as, vision, hearing and smell.

Frontal Center: The frontal center governs the encephalic cortex and therefore provides a foundation for sensory processing, control of the activity of the endocrine glands and administration of the nervous system in its entire organization, coordination, activity, and mechanism, starting from the sensorial neurons to the response mechanism executed by effector cells.

It is in the frontal center, contiguous to the crown center, that we find the various types of perception, which in the physical body, comprise sight, hearing, touch and the vast network of the processes of the mind that have to do with speech, learning, art and knowledge. It is responsible for integration, synthesis, reasoning, and for intellectual perception.

It is in in the frontal center that we possess the command of the endocrine center, which has to do with the psychic powers. It is made up of three pairs of intra-cranial ganglions. It gets intensely involved in mediumistic reception. It has a direct link to the pituitary gland, sensitizing all otorhinolaryngological and ophthalmologic regions, stimulating odors and other endocrine glands that increase hormone production.

In mediumship, it is the center of force that is activated during the manifestation of phenomena such as: clairvoyance, clairaudience and intuition. It also plays an important role in the exteriorization of ectoplasm for materializations and other phenomena in physical manifestations.

The frontal center is also in charge of the degree of control of the gesticulations during a trance communication. In magnetism, it plays a strong role in hypnosis as well as in memory regression. Through the frontal center a relation of control can be established or broken from the bond exerted by someone else.

The main function of this center of force is to develop the inner being and the intellectual and spiritual evolvement in the human being.

Laryngeal or Throat Center

Center of Creativity
<u>GLANDS:</u> Thyroid and Parathyroid. the thyroid, producing thyroxine, which controls the rate at which the body converts food into useful energy.
<u>LOCATED:</u> 3rd cervical - At the throat
<u>SYMPATHETIC PLEXUS:</u> Pharyngeal
<u>RAYS:</u> 16
<u>COLORS:</u> Color of the Moon, Violet-blue

RESPONSIBILITY: Speech, the respiratory system, the initial digestive process, and blood pressure.

Laryngeal Center: The laryngeal center, which presides over the vocal phenomena, includes the activities of the thymus, thyroid and the parathyroid. This center of force notably controls respiration and phonation. In the physical body it has two ganglions that supply the larynx and the base of the tongue, it also activates the larynx muscles and serves as a constrictor to the larynx and the vocal cords.

The influence of the sympathetic Plexus, which we can call pharyngeal, also provokes a very common phenomenon that makes the medium feel heaviness in that area, and then, is able to hear words before one pronounces them. The laryngeal center completely dominates the phonetic system, from the involuntary lung muscles to the controlled expulsion of air used in talking.

In mediumship, it plays an important role in the phenomena of trance communication. It is also very active in the exteriorization of ectoplasm. In magnetism, it is responsible for healing breath therapy.

The laryngeal center, which presides over the vocal phenomena, including the activities of the thymus, thyroid and the parathyroid.

Cardiac or Heart Center

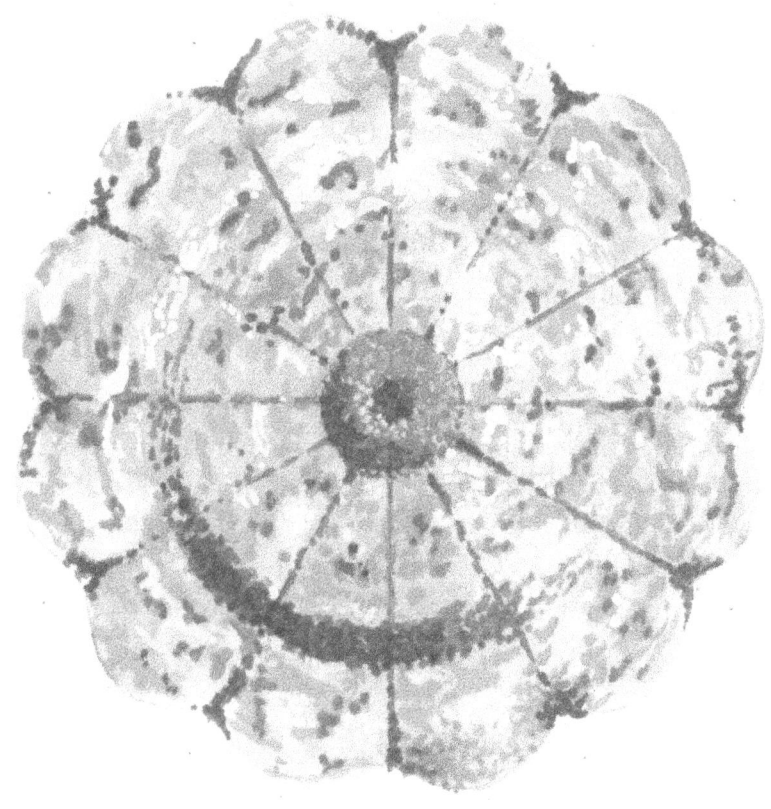

Center of Sentiment
GLAND: Thymus produces lymphocytes, which form a vital part of the body's immune response.
LOCATED: 8th cervical - Over the heart
SYMPATHETIC PLEXUS: Cardiac
RAYS: 12
COLORS: A glowing golden color

RESPONSIBILITY: The circulatory system, the control of the sentiments, and the nervous system.

Cardiac Center: It is located over the heart. It is related to the spiritual principle of being and governs the circulatory system. The cardiac center directs emotional behavior and the circulation of the elemental forces. It is the cardiac center that sustains the services of the emotions and overall equilibrium.

On less evolved beings, the vibrations from the Gastric Center, which transfers uncontrolled and inferior emotions to the Cardiac Center, affects it. In the physical body, it is located on the trachea bifurcation, unnerving the aorta, the lung artery, the heart and the pericardium. This center of force and its sympathetic plexus are greatly utilized during the passes. The Spiritual Mentors of the Center and the pass givers will link themselves through fluidic ties if the pass givers pray asking for their assistance during the task.

In mediumship, it acts in the assimilation of the emotional field of the communicating spirits. In magnetism, it utilizes subtle energies in the pass process. It also acts as an attenuator of the vibrations of the material energies and as a condenser in relation to the spiritual energies.

Gastric or Umbilical Center

Center of Vitality
GLAND: Pancreas and the outer adrenal glands
LOCATED: 8th thoracic - Over the navel
SYMPATHETIC PLEXUS: Solar Plexus
RAYS: 10
COLORS: Red and Green
RESPONSIBILITY: Feelings and emotions of various kinds, with the digestive processes, also, part of the metabolic system, stomach, and sympathetic nervous system.

Gastric Center: This is located in the area between the belly button and the stomach, it expresses emotions on a personal and human level. The gastric center, which is responsible for the digestive and absorptive processes of both dense and less dense nutrients that, in one form or another, correspond to the concentrated fluids gaining access to the physical organization.

It is used excessively by humankind causing it to be a very troubled center of force. In this level, passion influences and conditions human beings: their opinions, decisions and actions. Ethereally, if there is emotional immaturity involved, the cosmic energy will not flow to the cardiac center, but will remain blocked in this center of force. In the physical body, it is made up by two semi-biliary ganglions, right above the pancreas. It enervates the stomach, intestines, liver, etc.

In mediumship, it attracts suffering spirits and spirits of a dense vibration. In magnetism, it produces the greatest quantity of vital fluid that an organism normally produces for its self-maintenance, donation and exteriorization.

Splenic or Spleen Center

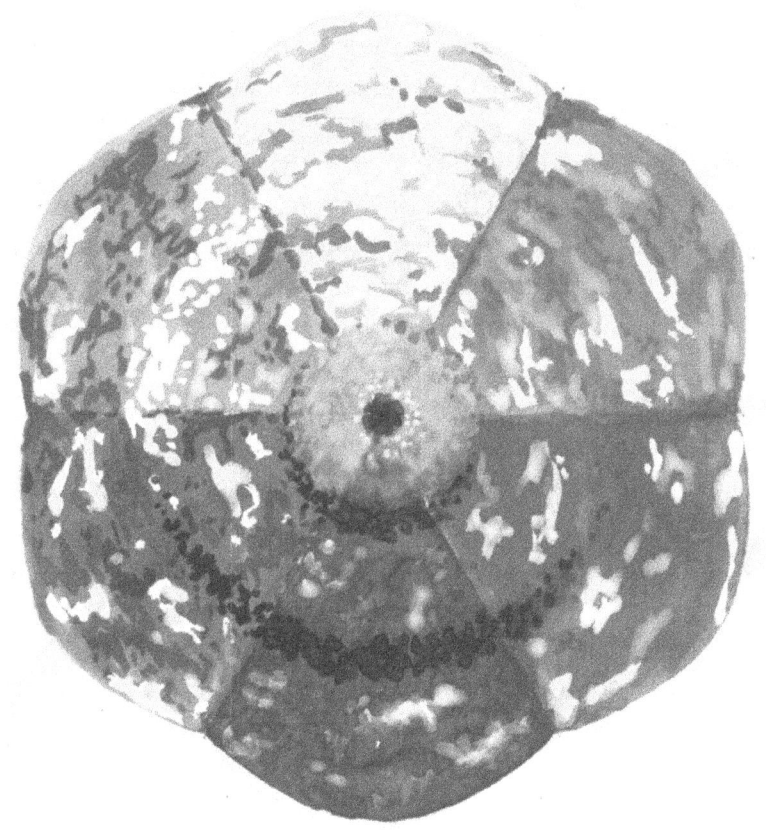

Center of the Equilibrium
GLAND: Pancreas secretes substances for the digestion of food, such as insulin.
LOCATED: 1st lumbar - Over the Spleen
SYMPATHETIC PLEXUS: Splenic
RAYS: 6
COLORS: Colors of the Rainbow

RESPONSIBILITY: The spleen, which is responsible for the formation and replacement of organic defenses through the circulation of blood. It is dedicated to the specialization, subdivision and dispersion of the vitality that comes to us from the Sun.

Splenic Center: The splenic center, in the dense body, is seated in the spleen and regulates the distribution and circulation adequate for the vital resources in every corner of the body. It is one of the centers of force responsible for the vitalization of the physical body, intensely absorbing energy and then distributing it.

The splenic center regulates the circulation of cosmic vital elements, which are eliminated through the pores after circulation. There are spirits who link themselves to the splenic center, intent on sucking vital energy from human beings. They are commonly called "vampires" because they thrive on our energy for their objectives. In the physical body, its sympathetic plexus is composed of lumbar nerves that reach the kidney. When the patient is under the control of vampire entities, certain signs of discomfort may be noticed around the lumbar and abdominal regions. Sometimes the patient may also feel shakiness in the legs, as well as excessive paleness and weakness.

In mediumship, it responds to the activities of the fluidic donations made by frail Spirits or Spirits with grave problems in their perispiritual body. In magnetism, it produces a great amount of vital fluid for the organic renewal, especially those pertaining to the reconstitution of organs, bones, etc.

Genesic or Root Center

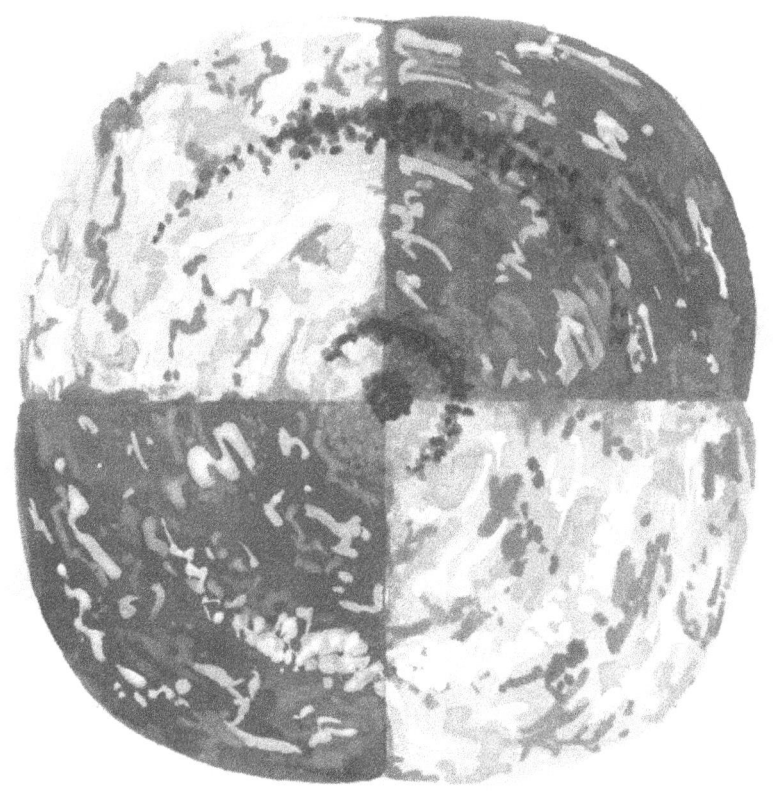

Center of the Equilibrium
GLAND: Reproductive Glands
LOCATED: 4th sacral – At the base of the Spine
SYMPATHETIC PLEXUS: Coccygeal
RAYS: 4
COLORS: Red and Orange
RESPONSIBILITY: The reproductive organs and all the resulting emotions related to them.

Genesic Center: The genesic center is the one that guides the modeling of new forms among humans and the establishment of creative stimuli towards work and relationships as well as a sense of fulfillment among the incarnate beings.

When this center of force is utilized excessively for the satisfaction of inferior pleasures, it becomes a factor of imbalance; when utilized with dignity and wisdom in the name of love, it represents the fundamental energy of life.

Physically, it corresponds to the Coccygeal Plexus, with six pairs of sacred nerves, from where the sciatic nerve extends to the legs. It regulates activities related to sex and reproduction.

In mediumship, the basic chakra liberates energies of vigorous magnetic attraction. In magnetism, it is the producer of dense energies.

CHAPTER 5

The Three Types of Passes

For purposes of classification, we normally divide the application of passes in three different categories:

- **Spiritual Pass**
- **Magnetic Pass**
- **Combined Pass (magnetic and spiritual)**

There are two types of fluid: magnetic and spiritual fluids. During the pass our efforts are assisted by Good Spirits who control the pass in its spiritual aspect as well as influence it magnetically. Magnetic pass, therefore, does not occur on its own. Theoretically, passes combine spiritual components under the control of Good Spirits and magnetic aspects accentuated according to the pass giver's own magnetic resources.

Spiritual Pass:
The Spirits give the Spiritual Pass to one or more people at the same time, with or without the assistance of a pass giver. In the case where the Spirits use the resources of a medium, they manipulate fluids used in this type of pass, even at a distance.

- **Spiritual Pass Giver**: Pass givers normally feel a gentle and agreeable sensation at the top of their head. They notice a circulation of subtle vibration and pleasant sensation coming over their body, especially circulating through their forehead, heart, lungs and upper part of their body. It proceeds uninterruptedly through the arms, reaching the hands and finally it is spread over the patient. At the end of the pass session pass givers feel no disagreeable sensation or fatigue.

Magnetic Pass:

The Magnetic Pass is transmitted by the pass givers, who provide their own personal magnetic fluids, using only their irradiating personal energy. It is extremely useful for organic, physical and perispiritual problems.

- **Magnetic Pass Giver:** The pass givers manifest clear signs of the magnetic process that their perispirit undergoes. The centers of force trigger the "fluidic production" that are felt in the physical body. In the majority of cases, the gastric center is the first and most powerful one in the emission of magnetic fluids; therefore, it is common to perceive sensations in the abdomen.

Combined Pass (magnetic and spiritual):

The Combined Pass uses both magnetic and spiritual fluids. It aims to assist in physical, perispiritual and spiritual problems.

- **Combined Pass Giver:** The pass givers perceive slight sensations of the above-mentioned types, depending on their sensitivity. If they do not possess a minimum amount of sensitivity, they will probably not register any special sensation. In this case, it does not mean that they are not transmitting magnetic fluids and that they should refrain from participating as magnetic pass givers.

The Process of Passes

Physical and moral imbalances effect our perispirit, either by aiding or inhibiting the process of organic equilibrium. The symptoms of an imbalance differ according to the type, source and duration of the pain or suffering, which can be mental, physical or both. We should understand these symptoms as alarm signals informing us of an emergency and of needing assistance to heal the body, Spirit or both. The assistance may be in the form of medicine, as pass, or a combination of both. The pass, as considered within Spiritism, can be helpful for both the body and the soul.

In the process of passes we have the following essential elements:

1. The patient: a person in need.
2. The pass giver: a person willing and able to help.
3. The Spiritual Benefactors: the directors and organizers of the process.

The pass process originates on the spiritual plane where highly qualified Spirits participate in manipulating fluids, thus ensuring that they are the most beneficial for each patient.

During the process, the pass givers, who have become attuned to the Spiritual Benefactors through prayer and through a correct mental attitude, become endowed with these fluidic resources.

Thus, good affinity enhances the pass givers' ability to absorb healthy fluids from the spiritual world, which are received through their crown center. The pass givers then transmit these fluids to the patient together with any vital fluid, thereby seeking to bring about an improvement in the patient's general well being. The transmission of fluids is usually carried out by placing their hands above the patient's head.

One of the reasons that the pass giver's hands are placed over the patient's head is because the crown center located on the top of the head, commands the function of all the other centers of force, and is responsible for the distribution of vital fluid throughout the entire nervous system. The healing fluids that are in close contact with the patient's perispirit are those closest to the patient's crown center. This center of force propels the fluids toward the ones where they are most needed and where they are absorbed. This process is no different from taking a pill that is digested in the stomach, but which is destined to alleviate a headache.

Psychical Force, Fluids and Magnetism

When talking about Magnetic Passes, it is noteworthy mentioning that "the study of spiritual phenomena has made known to us, states of matter and conditions of life that science had long ignored. We have learned that, beyond the gaseous state and even the radiant state discovered by W. Crookes, matter, which becomes unseen and imponderable, is found in increasingly subtle forms that we refer to as fluids. As it becomes rarefied, it acquires new properties, a power of increasing radiation, and becomes one of the forms of energy.

"There exists within each of us an invisible focal point whose radiations will vary in amplitude and intensity according to our mental dispositions. The will can impart special properties to them; and therein lies the secret of the healing power of magnetizers.

"In fact, it was to these latter that this force first revealed itself, in its therapeutic applications. Its nature was studied by Baron Karl von Reichenbach, who named it od, or odic force, whereas W. Crookes, for his part, was the first to measure its intensity.[17]

"Physical effects mediums can exteriorize abundant amounts of this force; however, we all possess it to varying degrees. It is by means of this force that the rising of tables off the ground, displacement of objects without visible contact, apport phenomena, direct writing on slates, etc. are made possible. Its action is present in all spirit manifestations.

"The emanations of the human body are luminous, colored with various hues, as reported by sensitives, whose sight they impress in the darkened room. Some mediums can see them even in full light, escaping from the hands of magnetizers. They were analyzed using the spectroscope, and their wavelengths were determined according to each color.

"These emanations form concentric layers around the individual, which constitute a kind of fluidic atmosphere. This is the

---

17 See W. Crookes, Researches in the Phenomena of Spiritualism (London: J. Burns, 1874), p. 62 et seq.; Karl Reichenbach, Researches on Magnetism ... (Trans. W. Gregory, London, Taylor, 1850), Part II, passim. Also, Prof. d'Arsonval, of the College of France, in a note presented at the Paris Academy of Sciences, on Dec. 28, 1903, said that, "The emission of rays by the nervous system may, under certain conditions, persist after the – at least apparent – death of the organism, and be increased by excitations of reflex origin." Further on, he adds: "I have reason to believe that unexpressed thought, one's attention and mental effort give rise to an emission of rays acting upon phosphorescence."

so-called aura of Occultists, or human photosphere. It explains the phenomenon of exteriorization of sensibility, established by numerous experiments made by Col. Rochas d'Aiglun, Dr. Luys, Dr. Paul Joire, etc.[18]

"By allowing a human being to act mentally upon another, without the help of the senses, it makes us better understand the action of the mind on a medium. Indeed, what humans can obtain, whose power and action are limited, hindered, and diminished, an intelligent being freed from the hindrances of coarse matter, will do all the better, and succeed in influencing a sensitive, inspiring him or her, and using him or her to accomplish its own views.

"Magnetism, taken in its general sense, is the use, under the name of fluids, of psychical force by those who are abundantly provided with it.

"The action of magnetic fluids is demonstrated by so numerous and convincing examples, that only ignorance or bad faith would deny their existence today.

"The will to relieve and heal, as mentioned earlier, lends curative properties to magnetic fluids. The remedy to our ills is in ourselves. Good, healthy individuals can act upon weak and suffering beings, regenerating them through breath blowing, the laying on of hands, and even by means of objects impregnated with his energy. The most usual action is by means of gestures, called

---

[18] See Rochas d'Aiglun, *L'Extériorization de la Sensibilité*, passim; Dr. J. Luys, "Phénomènes Produits par l'Action des Médicaments à Distance," in *L' Encéphale*, 7: 74–81, Paris, 1887. As early as 1860, Allan Kardec in The Spiritist Review – 1860 (New York: USSC, 2016), p. 129, affirmed that, according to the revelations made by the spirit of Dr. Vignal, our bodies emit luminous vibrations invisible to the material senses. That is what science has since confirmed. Therefore Spiritism has the merit of having been the first to propose, on this as on so many other points, theories of physics that science accepted only thirty years later, under the constant pressure of facts.

passes, which may be swift or slow, longitudinal or transverse, depending on the calming or stimulating effect one wishes to produce in the patient. This treatment should continue regularly, and sessions renewed every day, until the cure is complete.

"Ardent faith, willpower, prayer, and the evocation of higher powers, can give support both to the operator and the subject. When both are united in thought and heart, the healing action becomes more intense.

"The exaltation of faith, which causes a sort of dilation of the psychical being and makes it more accessible to the influx from above, which leads us to admit and allows us to explain some extraordinary cures carried out at places of pilgrimage and religious sanctuaries. There are numerous cases of cure backed by testimonies which are too important to be all rejected as doubtful. They are not exclusive to this or that religion; we find them indistinctly in the most diverse circles: Catholics, Orthodox, Muslims, Hindus, and others.

"When stripped of any theatricality and all ulterior motives, and practiced only for the sake of charitable love, magnetism becomes the medicine of the humble and believers, of the family man and the mother of their children, in short, of all those who know how to love. Its application is within easy reach. It requires only self-confidence and faith in the infinite power that radiates strength and life everywhere. Like Christ and the apostles, like the saints, prophets and magi, each and every one of us can lay on hands and heal, if we have love for our fellow human beings, and an ardent will to bring relief to them."[19]

---

19 Excerpted from the book *Into the Unseen* by Leon Denis, Healing, pages 215 and 216

CHAPTER 6

The Pass Giver

THE MOST FREQUENTLY ASKED QUESTIONS about passes are:

- Who can be a pass giver?
- How do I know if I can be a pass giver?

The answer to these questions is two-sided because both physical and moral requirements must be analyzed.

First, someone who is physically unwell or weak is not in condition to donate vital fluid to another person. Although these fluids are replenished in the process of the pass, anyone who is in need of vital fluid should be a "patient" and not a "pass giver." Some people have a greater capacity to absorb and store vital fluids than others and, as a result, enjoy greater vitality. This accumulation can occur unconsciously or as a result of a humble request through prayer. Second, having established that a person is physically well and in condition to transmit vital fluids to a patient, we must also consider the moral and mental condition of the proposed pass giver because this also affects the quality of the spiritual fluids he or she will be transmitting.

When we remember that the flux of fluids from the pass giver to the patient is established and maintained by the pass giver's willpower, we understand how important it is that the pass giver actively participates. The whole process begins with setting up the contact between the pass giver and the Spiritual Benefactors through prayer. Therefore, someone who is not able or willing to pray is not a proper instrument for the task.

Pass givers are simply a channel for the spiritual fluids, which have been manipulated and offered by the Spiritual Benefactors. Therefore, it is necessary for this channel to be as clear as possible so that the fluids are not contaminated.

A "clean channel" must not only provide a physical body that is well, but also one that is not intoxicated. This channel must also have healthy and charitable thoughts, which do not allow any inferior thought-patterns to interfere in the process. No pass giver is expected to be perfect, as this is still an inferior world, but a constant conscientious effort towards perfection must exist.

In order to maintain good physical health the body requires proper food, regular exercise, rest and the avoidance of all harmful and intoxicating substances. In order to maintain good thoughts, it is necessary to practice Christian virtues, to make a daily effort towards moral improvement and to study Spiritism, which offers a means of putting these into practice.

Above all, every potential pass giver must understand the great responsibility that one is undertaking as the patient is placing oneself trustingly in another's hands. Furthermore, the potential pass giver is also undertaking a commitment with the group where the pass will take place. They will also be counting on the pass giver to be available for the task on pre-arranged days.

Finally, pass givers must cultivate humility and remember that they are solely a channel or instrument of the pass and can always be substituted without prejudice to the patient. In parallel, pass givers must cultivate love for their neighbor by trying to offer their best always and making a continuous effort to be a better person.

Recommendations to The Pass Giver

The Spirit Andre Luiz, in his book *"In the Domain of Mediumship,"* informs us that goodwill is the basic quality that the medium must possess. In addition, one must also have the following qualities:

1. Doctrinal knowledge and balanced behavior.
   * The pass giver is the incarnate that stands in front of the patient and represents the magnetizing Protecting Spirit, in addition to transmitting a message of love. The absence of study on the part of the incarnate represents stagnation.
   * The pass giver's cultural achievements will improve his/her psychological resources, which will facilitate a better receptivity to the recommendations and guidance received from the Spiritual Instructors.
2. Good mental and physical health.
3. Emotional balance.
4. Control over thoughts and feelings. One must also feel love for one's neighbors, have a good understanding of life and an unshakable faith.
5. Desire for inner reform.
6. Exercise self-control.
7. Faith and a deep trust in Divine power.

But apart from these requirements above, there are impediments that must be avoided by the pass giver:

1. Emotional imbalance.
2. Excessive lamenting, hatred and anger.
3. Passionate rage, short temper, discourtesy, envy, jealousy, vanity, pride, and intolerance.
4. Uneasiness, mental depression, loud laughter and hysterical crying for no significant reason.
5. Lack of moderation, cursing, being ironic and intransigent.
6. Bad habits such as: smoking, taking drugs, the use of alcohol, and deviation from correct behavior.

CHAPTER 7

The Patient

As stated in the chapter 3, the process of the pass has three essential elements: the Spiritual Benefactors, the patient and the pass giver. The Spiritual Benefactors are always present because they are the directors of the work. Furthermore, by comparing the remaining two elements, we can conclude that the patient must exist, whether present or absent, as otherwise there is no need for the pass session to occur. When the patient is not present in the Spiritist Center the pass is called "absentee pass."

Although pass givers are an important element in the process of the pass, they must beware of assuming pride or assuming themselves to be indispensable to the work, as the Spiritual Benefactors can heal the patient directly, if required.

If this is the case, why is it necessary for the patient to participate in the pass in a regular session at a Spiritist Center? This is because, being an incarnate, the pass giver can help the patient by transmitting spiritual fluids as well as part of his or her own vital fluid. This is what, in some cases, the patient most urgently needs.

Considering that the patient is seeking assistance, they should receive orientation either prior to or after the pass as to how one can best help oneself through prayer and a change of attitude, as well as praying for others in need. When a reverent state of mind can be easily achieved, it is possible for the patient to heal oneself if they are in need of passes and are unable to go to a Spiritist Center. This is called "self-pass." Generally, however, the results of the pass will depend on having both, the presence of the Spiritual Benefactors and of the patient.

These results fall into three categories:

- **Beneficial:** Pass givers' vital fluid depends on their state of health, and the spiritual fluids they are able to assimilate depends on their affinity with the Good Spirits. This affinity is needed for the pass to have beneficial results.

    Simultaneously, the patient must be receptive to the pass process and well disposed to spiritual improvement. If the patient is unwilling to collaborate in the general process, the results are temporary. This is especially true if the patient makes no effort to lead a Christian life.
- **Harmful:** If pass givers are in a precarious state of health, or their organism is intoxicated due to vices such as smoking, drinking, drugs, etc., or are in a state of spiritual imbalance due to sentiments of revolt, vanity, pride, anger, desperation, worry, mistrust, etc., they are not in any condition to transmit the pass.

    If in addition, the patient's defenses are almost non-existent and he or she is unable to neutralize the torrent of inferior and gross fluids being transmitted by the careless pass giver, the pass received can only be harmful.
- **Null:** If, despite the aid being offered by a well-prepared pass giver, the patient places oneself in an impenetrable position due to disbelief, aversion, or a frivolous attitude, etc., the pass is voided. The patient will not be able to

absorb the spiritual fluids, thus becoming nullified. Here we can reiterate the need for the patient to collaborate by being receptive and also by changing their mental outlook so as to be healed.

The pass can also be nullified by the patient who receives gross or negative fluids. This occurs when receiving the pass from an unprepared pass giver, or in an improper environment.

CHAPTER 8

When the Pass is Helpful

SPIRITISM TEACHES THE LAW OF Cause and Effect, wherein each of us must face the consequences of our actions, whether these actions were in the past or present life. Each person must go through trials and atonements, as well as learn new lessons. This brings pain and suffering - emotional, spiritual and physical. Spiritism also teaches: "Without Charity there is no Salvation;" therefore, it is essential that assistance be offered to all in need. This is God's infinite love and mercy in action, which gives us opportunity to practice charity that is vital to our progress.

If it is our Christian duty to help those in need, we must then ask, when is it most appropriate? In terms of passes, should we therefore offer assistance anywhere, anytime, whatever the situation? Let us then remember that there is a time and a place for everything.

Let us now look when the pass is most appropriate.

* **In Relation to the Patient:**

There are many ways of helping a person in need. Sometimes a constant renewal of energies (through the pass) may be seen to have no effect. This is perhaps due to the fact that after the pass the individual was not advised of the necessary accompanying guidance, which should always encourage the individual to participate in one's own process of recuperation. This guidance should never be given during the actual pass. The pass giver may be of assistance, but the patient must also fulfill one's part.

- **Passes May be Administered When:**

The patient requests passes with the understanding that he abides by the rules of the regular Pass Sessions of the Center or Group.

Passes are advantageous in all cases, whether it is physical, emotional or spiritual, if the patient is disposed to collaborate. However, there are some instances in which the patient's participation is impossible, such as: in cases of epileptic seizures, obsession or spiritual attachment, violent fevers, etc. There are also occasional cases of hypnosis or deep somnambulism in which the patient needs to be awakened.

Passes are of great benefit as a restorer of energy and as a complement to all medical treatment. It can be essential as a means of repairing prior problems caused by modern medical medicine. It is also beneficial in preparation for surgery or other special treatment recommended by the medical profession, as well as the approach of either a reincarnation or a discarnate process.

In cases of obsessions, there are specific instructions that apply, which are discussed in the next chapter.

It is noteworthy to mention that passes are not intended to substitute any necessary medical treatment.

CHAPTER 9

When Passes Are Not Convenient

IN CASES OF OBSESSION OR spiritual attachment never give pass without first consulting with the Director of the Center or Group, bearing in mind that in these cases there is need for additional preparation, special precautions as well as a team of pass givers.

- Never give passes when there has been no preparation in the form of prayer or away from the Spiritist Center, a reading from the Gospel and a message, in the ambient where the pass is to take place.
- Never give pass for the mere convenience of the patient, nor when there are no prepared pass givers available, other than at regular times.
- Always use common sense in all matters of this nature remembering that it is in the responsibility of all the mediums to be prudent, disciplined and responsible at all times.
- Never give pass when feeling unwell, either physically, emotional or spiritually.

As for this last point, it is rare for us to say that we are perfectly well, so we must guard against exaggerating of our own limitations for giving passes. If we have the "flu", are coughing, have a sore throat, or if we feel excessively tired, nervous, upset, stressed, depressed, have a toothache, a stomach ache, feel unusually sad, desiring to weep or become angry without sufficient reason, then we can be assured that all is not as it should be. In such cases the pass giver must excuse oneself from giving passes on that day.

If the pass giver has a chronic health condition that is not contagious and is not necessarily disturbing the rhythm of that day, so that one can pray normally, feel happy and uplifted, there would be no impediment to perform the task of the pass.

Do not let your enthusiasm and joy over giving passes override your judgment and sense of responsibility. If a pass giver is not in good condition, it is better for the patient and for the pass giver to refrain from giving passes on that particular day.

If there is any doubt in one's mind, the pass giver can always ask for advice from the directors from the Spiritist Center.

CHAPTER 10

Where Passes May Be Performed

MOST APPROPRIATE PLACE FOR PASSES:
THE MOST APPROPRIATE LOCATION FOR the pass is within a Spiritist Center or Group since it is there that an effort is made to maintain a constant environment of spirituality, as well as being a place populated by Spiritual Benefactors who specialize in this work.

However, location is not the only point to be considered. Punctuality, dedication, assiduousness, and seriousness on the part of the incarnate workers within the Center is crucial. Also, the team of pass givers are of equal importance.

Wherever possible, use a small room, or, as a second alternative, a regular location allocated to the service of passes on given days, at specified times.

INADEQUATE PLACES FOR PASSES:
Any place where there is improper or insufficient ventilation, fumes from smoking, alcohol usage or a large gathering of people, where there might be sarcastic or irreverent people in the vicinity, is inappropriate to the pass. No goodness can be derived in a polluted atmosphere.

This also includes places frequented by large groups of people in transit, any ambient where there is loud noise or where there is any form of mental pollution. These restrictions omit the majority of public places other than a Spiritist Center.

Generally, it is not advisable to heal in a private home, be it yours or any other, as there are discordant vibrations frequently encountered, as well. However, there will be occasions when this becomes necessary. In this case it is imperative to prepare the room thoroughly by reading the Gospel and offering prayer. In addition it is necessary to utilize a team of pass givers with a minimum of three well-qualified and experienced persons.

Bearing all this in mind, we must be reminded that above all, we must always have a charitable attitude. Therefore, in cases of an unexpected emergency, special needs and circumstances, the pass giver of true faith, conviction and discipline will find it possible to render assistance even in what would ordinarily be considered unsatisfactory. For the dedicated pass giver there will always be protection and assistance available from the Spiritual Benefactors.

Nevertheless, pass givers must never overuse this permission, because they would soon lose the "back up" of the trustworthy Spiritual Helpers. Therefore, we must be cautious in evaluating what one may call "an emergency."

Organization within a Center:

The most adequate location to be chosen for this work is within the Spiritist Center. As already mentioned, a separate room dedicated exclusively to this work is ideal. When this is not possible, a quiet place can be screened off, preferably at the back of the room, away from curious eyes. All sessions for passes must be pre-arranged and held at a fixed time.

There should always be a person experienced in passes, who has received the specific orientation, designated to supervise the "work team" in case of any emergency or if special attention is required.

Regular seminars of passes should be held to train newcomers for this work, as well as to offer opportunity for established pass givers to review the basic principles of the pass.

Before any "session" begins, it is essential that the ambient be properly prepared through prayer. Water can be provided in small disposable cups. Music for the ambient can be also utilized, provided that it is adequately chosen and played softly.

Preparation of pass givers:
Preparation for the pass is a daily occurrence, whether the person is scheduled for the pass on that day or not. The pass giver must work diligently and persistently on their personal inner reform and evolvement with the aim of spiritual elevation. Clean spiritual fluids will be sullied if passed through a soiled channel. So there is a great responsibility in becoming a pass giver!

The most adequate Spiritual Companions for this task will only work through those persons who offer the correct vibrations of a corresponding nature, who are prepared, punctual, assiduous, responsible, work hard at their inner reform and who hold reverence for God, Jesus and the Spiritual Benefactors. Also, these workers must make an intentional effort to love their fellow beings and be willing to commit themselves for this blessed work. Other requirements for the prospective pass giver are: to observe a balanced diet, regular exercise and sufficient rest (chapter 3 – Recommendations to the pass giver).

NOTE: A person who smokes, is a habitual drinker, a drug user, is frequently irritable, easily roused to anger, suffers bouts of depression, constantly uses bad language, excessively committed to sex, frequents undesirable places, or who generally lives a frivolous life, is not an adequate candidate to become a pass giver as long as they are unable to change their life-style and habits.

Preparation on the day of passes:

Extra care is needed on this day. Upon awakening the usual prayer should be followed by a short reading of the Gospel in order to commence the day.

Care with personal hygiene is always necessary, but special care is required on this day. You should not fast, but neither should you overeat. The pass giver must only eat foods that are easily digested. It is impossible to have a full dinner and then go giving passes! The entire digestive system will be occupied with digestion, which could interfere with the quality and capacity to serve as a good, clear channel. So, only a light snack is recommended prior to going to the session.

It is also necessary to observe your attitude carefully on that day. Particular care should be observed to avoid attracting inferior Spirits, which will nullify or intoxicate the pass given by the pass giver.

All attire should be very clean and comfortable, do not wear tight clothing. Also, the use of comfortable shoes is recommended. Be sure that you are not too warm or too cold. Avoid using noisy jewelers, pagers, cellular phones, alarm watches, etc., during the session.

During the day, pass givers should be, as much as possible, praying for their own protection and for the assistance of any spirit that may be close by. A short reading from the Gospel and a prayer before leaving home on the way to the Center is advisable.

If at all possible, a short rest is also recommended before starting out. If the pass giver is coming directly from work, then rest, pray or read on the way in.

The pass giver must cultivate a humble attitude on this day and seek to maintain peace and harmony with everyone they come in contact with, even those who desire to become argumentative.

Upon arrival at the Center:
Upon arrival at the Center, the pass givers must ask themselves the question: Am I in the right condition to give passes today?

Long conversations with companions upon arrival is not advised. This is a pleasure to be reserved for after the task has been completed. There is need to maintain a state of seclusion and constant prayer prior to the beginning of the meeting.

Pay close attention to the teachings during the lecture or study and then be ready for the special prayer for preparation.

When the pass session is about to begin (after the pass givers have assumed their positions), the pass giver must then maintain a state of prayer and evolved thoughts. A state of trance is not allowed; however, there will be a very slight "altered state of consciousness" during the period of concentration.

The pass giver must be attentive when someone approaches and sits on their chair. When the patients are seated all the pass givers begin the pass together.

Once the patient has received the pass, the pass givers continue in concentration and contact with the Spiritual Benefactors, keeping their eyes closed until the next patient approaches the chair. This procedure continues until all guests have been cared for

During the closing prayer, the pass givers should offer their own personal prayer of thanks for the opportunity to be of service, and for the protection and collaboration received from the Spirits, who allowed the task to be accomplished successfully.

At the close of the session it is proper to maintain the spiritual ambient, as long as possible, and to direct conversation to elevated topics.

CHAPTER 11

Practical Guidance

1. Pass givers may take up their position at the rear or at the side of the patient. When the pass begins they may continue to stand in that position or may move around and stand in front of the patient. If this is the case, the pass giver must quietly move to the side when the pass is completed, while awaiting the arrival of the next patient.
2. Hands should be held approximately 6 to 12 inches above the head of the patients. This position is to be maintained as long as the pass givers feel the "pass vibration" flowing through their fingers and palms of their hands (that's assuming the Spiritist Center is using the technique of laying on of hands). Then slowly and carefully the hands should be lowered to the sides.
3. At no time should the pass givers' hand touch the patients, or even brush against their hair. This will cause a "shock" sensation to both the patient and the pass giver, which is disruptive for both parties.
4. Every pass session must have a director observing the task from the physical aspect. This person should be responsible for calling the correct number of patients at any given time.

5. There is also a need for a person to distribute the magnetized water (see item 13.2) after the pass session is completed (providing the Spiritist Center follows this procedure).
6. When the pass is carried out in an adjoining room, the door of this room is closed before the pass is begun and re-opened when each patient has been attended.
7. When all the patients have received the pass, the final prayer of thanks is given. This prayer should be short and precise. However, it is essential during this prayer to acknowledge the team of spiritual workers and to offer them our thanks. We may also ask for assistance with our own struggles toward progress and personal inner reform. Remember that true prayer comes from the heart, with deep sentiment, love and humility. We should add sincere feelings of immense gratitude for being permitted to take part in the task of giving passes.

CHAPTER 12

Absentee Pass

ABSENTEE PASS IS A TYPE of pass that is carried out in the absence of the patient. There are many cases in which the patient is physically unable to go to the pass session, because of distance involved or because the patient is bed-ridden. Sometimes it may be the case of someone who is in dire need but does not believe in Spiritism or in any other belief. Therefore, Absentee Pass makes it possible to be of assistance to anyone in need, either physically or spiritually, whether they are believers or not, or whether they know what we are involved in or not.

Let us remember that there is no distance too great for the positive action of the pass. The action of the Superior Spirits is not hindered or infringed by distances on Earth. They can act upon and cure even from the farthest regions of the planet.

This process is usually carried out in conjunction with the Mediumship Development Session. At a pre-arranged time especially reserved for this purpose, the names of those patients needing this type of assistance are called out individually and the group spends a few moments in concentrated prayer, directing their thoughts exclusively to each person, as their name is said. This creates a greater concentration of energies in their direction, the energies are multiplied according to the number of people joined in prayer and not, as is usually done, by the length of time dedicated to each name.

However, one cannot overlook the importance of the psychological effect of the patient's presence in a mediumistic environment or of the presence of the pass-giver at one's side. In this case there are two important elements enhancing the effectiveness of the treatment by way of passes. The psychological effect resulting from the induced stimulus on the patient's presence in an environment of people genuinely interested in assisting him or her, which leads him or her to feel secure and confident in himself or herself. This is a psychic reaction (of the patient's soul), therefore psychologically recognized in Psychology as "group stimulation," in which the loss of heart derived from solitude is overcome.

CHAPTER 13

The Pass Outside Of The Spiritist Center

THE PASS MAY BE GIVEN away from the Center when specially organized for that specific purpose.

1. TEAM OF MOBILE PASS GIVERS:
It is first necessary to organize a Team of Mobile Pass Givers. It is best to form a list of local pass givers who are available to answer calls to give passes at irregular times. Each team should not have less than three pass givers, including the director, and not more than six.

These teams should receive special orientation and given instruction as to the work routine to be applied, as well as being made well aware of the various difficulties that might arise in these circumstances.

2. PASSES AT HOME:
Passes at home are offered only to those people who are physically unable to visit a Center. Apart from the person who is to receive the pass, no other family members should be allowed to remain in the room, so as to avoid any break in vibratory harmony.

The procedure followed is customary. First it is necessary to prepare the ambient by means of a short prayer, a reading from *"The Gospel According to Spiritism"* followed by another prayer to completely create an appropriate ambient before the service of pass begins.

The reading should always be taken from *"The Gospel According to Spiritism,"* followed by a few words of explanation by the director of the Team, if he or she is so inspired. At this point it is not advisable to allow discussion or questions. If the patient wishes to ask a question, they must wait until the pass has been completed. In addition to the Gospel, a message from a doctrinal book may also be read. In total, about fifteen minutes is usually sufficient to begin to form a good vibratory ambient.

Then, the Team director will indicate the positions for the pass givers to assume and may either offer the pass prayer himself or designate one of the Team members to offer it. Among other things, this prayer must renew the request for protection, and call for the presence of the Spiritual Benefactors, having first offered the services of the pass givers as channels for the pass. At this point it is important that the person offering the prayer has an awareness of the formation of the ambient so as to be able to judge when it is appropriate to terminate the prayer and begin the actual process of the pass. Remember that in a home ambient, it is usually necessary to work harder to prepare a correct vibratory field than when the pass is at the Spiritist Center.

When the pass is over a closing prayer is offered. At this moment it is suggested that the patient be asked to offer thanks, provided that the patient has a habit of praying. When in doubt, it is better that the Team director offers this prayer, or else designate a Team member to close the procedure. Finally, the patient is offered a small cup of magnetized water.

3. PASSES IN PUBLIC PLACES:
What is meant by this is such places as public halls or theaters, etc., where the pass givers will be surrounded by members of the public and be unable to effectively isolate themselves. Therefore, it is not advisable to give passes under these circumstances.

We are well aware of the power of thought and this can work against us. As rapidly as the pass givers try to create a good ambient, the onlookers, having varied thought patterns, would immediately interrupt all attempts to have a healthy ambient around a patient. Even more importantly, the curious observers and often the incredulous stares would inevitably cause the penetration of negative fluids, which could cause great harm to both patient and the pass giver alike. What should be positive healthy pass fluids would become negative and an even destructive interference.

4. PASSES IN HOSPITALS AND PRISONS:
These are places in great need, but are also places where facilities for the pass are not readily available. Nevertheless, pass givers have been called upon to work in this type of ambient, at the request of patients or prisoners.

Whenever possible, a secluded place must be used. To apply passes in a hospital is perhaps even more difficult than a prison! It is frequently necessary to disguise the act of giving passes in a hospital, the type of pass being offered is usually frowned upon or prohibited. The pass under these circumstances is perhaps better done through ABSENTEE PASS, rather than creating a disturbance within a hospital.

In a prison there are more possibilities. A request through the Warden of the Prison may be arranged for the pass, or perhaps even an opportunity may arise, cleared by the Governor, for study meetings and passes within the confines of the prison. In this latter possibility, an appropriate room could be arranged for the pass therapy.

However, in all probability it would be exceedingly difficult to take a team of Pass Givers into a prison! Therefore, it is recommended that unless a team of Pass Givers can be present, this task should not be attempted.

5. **EMERGENCIES:**
Within the Center: The person "taken over" by a spirit should be offered immediate and appropriate assistance. In case of sickness, call an ambulance and continue the pass until help arrives.

If at any time during the pass the patient begins to go into a trance state, the pass giver must continue the pass and double their efforts at prayer for both the patient and the spirit trying to communicate. It is essential to call upon the Benefactors to envelop the spirit, while at the same time the pass giver continues to send out love to both parties. At the onset the pass giver must also quietly advise the patient not to concentrate, but rather, to open his eyes, so as to not allow the spirit to take over.

Remember in these cases it is primarily the responsibility of the supervisor to deal with both patient and spirit. The main task for pass givers is in increasing their effort at prayer and having loving thoughts directed to the spirit, while maintaining close contact with the Benefactors.

Outside the Center: We need to remember that without charity there is no salvation. Situations of genuine emergency may present themselves to the lone pass giver from time to time. On verifying that it is a true case of emergency, and that no other help is available, it is possible to offer passes but only after a brief prayer (through elevated thoughts to the Benefactors) without the usual preparations. We stress, however, the importance of verifying that is a true emergency.

These situations usually arise when no one else is present, except for the person in need. In such a case we do not need to fear any negative influences from the public. It will be necessary to maintain fervent (silent) prayer during the pass, and offer a verbal prayer of thanks afterward.

CHAPTER 14

The Service Of "Spiritual Passes"[20]

WE ENTERED AND FOUND OURSELVES in a soothing and luminous ambient.

An elderly gentleman and a respectable lady took notes in a small notebook. Spirits involved in healing services surrounded them.

Indicating the two mediums, our mentor informed us:

"These are Clara and Henrique, who are dedicated to the task of rendering assistance under the guidance of spirit friends."

"Why is this place so radiant?" – ventured Hilario with curiosity.

"In this room," explained Aulus affectionately, "we perceive sublime mental emanations of the majority of those who seek magnetic assistance with love and trust. Here we possess a kind of inner altar created by the thoughts, prayers and aspirations of those who approach us with their best intentions."

We did not have time for a long conversation.

---

20 An excerpt from the book *In the Domain of Mediumship*, chapter 17, from the spirit Andre Luiz, received through automatic writing by Francisco C. Xavier. Published by SAB, 2013.

Clara and Henrique, now in prayer, became surrounded by a halo of light. They looked as if they were almost separated from their body and they appeared to be in direct contact with the benefactors present. Naturally, they themselves were not aware of this.

Serene and self-assured, they absorbed the invigorating energies into the depth of their souls. They knew that prayer kept them in communication with invisible and profound source of luminous energy.

Standing shoulder-to-shoulder afflicted people stood murmuring in front of the closed door waiting for the preparations to finish.

The two mediums, however, appeared to be spiritually distant, enveloped by the group of fraternal Spirits, registering their instructions through intuitive resources.

From the radiations of Henrique's magnetism one could immediately perceive his spiritual superiority over his companion. Of the two, he was the leading figure. Because of this, positioned at his side was the spirit guide responsible for the task ahead.

Aulus embraced him affectionately and introduced him to us.

Brother Conrado, our new friend, embraced us warmly. He informed us that the service would be open to us so that we could learn what we might from it.

Our mentor invited us to be comfortable and authorized us to direct to Conrado whatever questions we had in mind.

Hilario, who at no time held his spontaneity, respectfully began his questioning:

"Brother Conrado, do you come here frequently?"

"Yes, the Institution services the sick two nights a week."

"Only to the incarnates that are ill?"

"Not at all. We take care of the needy of whatever nature."

"Can you rely on many to cooperate?"

"We are a team of helpers, according to the organization established by mentors in the Superior Spheres."

"Do you mean that in a Spiritist center, such as this one, there are spirit collaborators enrolled as doctors and nurses just like in an ordinary hospital on Earth?"

"Exactly. We are all far from spiritual perfection and our success depends upon experience, time, accuracy and responsibility from the faithful worker toward the obligations assumed. The Law cannot belittle the lines of logic."

"What about the mediums? Are they always the same ones?"

"Yes! In justifiable situations they can be replaced, although there may be problems that result from adjusting to the new influences."

My colleague directed a questioning glance toward the incarnate companions that remained in prayers and continued:

"Do our friends prepare themselves for the task through prayers?"

"Without a doubt. Prayer produces prodigious forces from the vigorous mental current it attracts. Through prayer, Clara and Henrique expel from their own interior world the gloomy remnants gathered during their daily circle of struggle. They then absorb from our plane the renewing substances with which they replenish themselves with in order to work effectively, in favor of their neighbor. In this way they offer help and end up being helped in return."

"Does this mean that they should not worry about becoming exhausted?"

"Not at all. Just as we, they do not appear here under the pretense of being the grantors of benefits, but rather, as beneficiaries who receive in order to give. Prayer, along with the recognition of our small merits, makes us humble links in a chain of assistance that originates in the Higher Spheres. Those of us in this room who are consecrated to the evangelical mission under Jesus' inspiration are somewhat like an electric outlet that allows the flow of a force that is not our own to produce energy and light."

Hilario smiled, satisfied with the clear explanation.

Conrado tapped Henrique's shoulders in order to remind him of the work schedule. The medium, in spite of not registering the gesture through a physical sensation, he immediately walked over to the door and opened it to the sufferers.

A large group of incarnates and discarnates congregated at the entrance, as the personnel of the center guided their movements.

When Conrado began his tasks, we rejoined our mentor.

Both mediums got to work.

Patients of all kinds entered the room with great hope and after being attended to left displaying signs of comfort. Clara and Henrique's hands radiated luminous sparks that provided vigor and well-being to the patients.

In most cases, they did not have to touch the patient's body directly. Magnetic resources applied at close range penetrated the aura of the sick, causing sudden changes.

The pass-givers were like two human batteries that, upon contact with Brother Conrado and his collaborators, were able to emit a variety of rays flowing from their hands after passing over their heads. The sight was truly fascinating due to the display of lights.

Hilario, upon noting this, asked our mentor:

"Why does the energy transmitted by our spirit friends pass first through the mediums' heads?"

"Even here," answered Aulus, "we cannot underestimate the importance of the mind. Thought plays a decisive role in healing. If the medium does not have faith and good will, he or she will not succeed in receiving the friendly Spirits who work upon these areas."

"However, there are many people who also are endowed with magnetic energy but unconcerned with morality!" I pondered.

"Yes," agreed the mentor, "you are referring to the common hypnotizers who are often bearers of exceptional energy. Their demonstrations are beautiful, impressive and convincing, but they work mainly in the sphere of pure phenomena without any edifying purposes in the spiritual field. Remember, Andre, that everyone has magnetic potential but it is expressed in different ways."

"Yet such professionals can also heal!" said my companion furthering my observations.

"Yes, they can also heal, but accidentally. When the patient is worthy of spiritual assistance, spiritual friends intervene to assist he or she. However, those that take advantage of this fountain of energy and exploit it for their personal gain, generally debase themselves interfering with unknown forces. They violate these forces, guided solely by vanity or an inferior ambition. They frequently encounter entities, with which they are attuned, submerging, thereby, in difficult situations that we will not go into now. If their character is too weak to pose a barrier to vicious influences, they end up devoured by energies stronger than theirs. There are an immense number of powerful spiritual hypnotizers who, through their ignorance and cruelty, are the initiators of the most afflictive cases of obsession."

After a pause, he smiled and added: "In nature, the serpent possesses the greatest hypnotic power."

"Then to heal, certain attitudes of the spirit are indispensable?" asked Hilario.

"Without a doubt we cannot succeed without a noble heart and a pure mind exercising love, humility, and a living faith, in order that the rays of the Divine Will can penetrate and flow from us for the benefit of others. To heal effectively, this is pivotal."

"Nonetheless, for a task of this nature, would we not require people who have made special studies?"

"It is important to clarify," said Aulus with conviction, "that regardless of the task, lack of study means stagnation. Every collaborator who resists learning, refusing to incorporate new knowledge, fatally condemns oneself to activities of a lower level. But regarding the magnetic assistance such as the kind offered here, the task is of pure solidarity, and requires an ardent desire to aid, under the invocation of prayer. Every prayer born of sincerity and a well-fulfilled duty, with moral respectability and clean sentiments, bears an incommensurable power. Therefore, all dignified and devoted person can with the aid of a prayer attract the sympathy of the venerable magnetizers of the Spirit Plane, who then will utilize him or her to promote goodness. We are not talking about the practice of showy hypnotism, but a place of healing, where mediums transmit the benefits that they receive, without presuming themselves to be the originators of healing. Wherever humility and love surge, Divine assistance is sure and immediate."

The healing task was proceeding effectively and peacefully, requiring our attention.

Clara and Henrique, who were under the providential assistance of Conrado and his collaborators, affectionately greeted the patients who entered two at a time.

Cruel executioners accompanied the obsessed individuals; however, as the mediums applied their hands over the cortical region, the perpetrators immediately moved away. Unfortunately the majority of them right away reunited with their victims after the treatment.

Reviewing our observations, we saw that some of the patients had not achieved even a minimum of improvement. Magnetic radiations were not penetrating their organic vehicles.

This phenomenon prompted Hilario to ask why.

"They lack confidence," clarified the mentor.

"Is faith indispensable, then, for them to receive the assistance they require?"

"Oh yes! In photography we require the photographic plate to hold the image, and with electricity we need a wire that can conduct the current. In spiritual assistance, the one in need requires faith to present a "favorable tension." We are not referring to religious fanaticism or to the blind faith of ignorance, but rather to an attitude of inner assurance, with reverence and submission to the Divine Laws, in whose wisdom and love we seek support. Without devotion and respect, we cannot fixate the imponderable resources that are offered to us for our own good. A heart that scorns at faith creates thick layers of ice around the soul."

Hilario became quiet, reflecting on the simple and beautiful lesson.

To help us towards the goal of our study, Aulus allowed us to observe the treatment directly. We agreed that it would be interesting to examine one of the cases before us. He approached an elderly lady who had just entered seeking assistance, and with Conrado's permission, he suggested that we examine her as attentively as possible.

The lady, while awaiting her encounter with Clara, stood with great difficulty. Her stomach was distended and her face showed pain.

"Look at liver," Aulus said.

The organ was dilated: a characteristic of people who suffer from cardiac failure. The hepatic cells appeared as a vast beehive working with enormous difficulty. The congested gall bladder brought my attention to the intestines. The bile, under compression had reached the vessels, and was compromising the blood. The blocked bile duct made the diagnosis easy. A cursory examination of the ocular mucous membrane confirmed my impression: all evidence indicated the woman suffered from jaundice.[21]

N.T: jaundice - a yellowing of the skin, usually showing up in the whites of the eyes, fingernails, and other lightly pigmented parts of the body surface. There are three main causes: 1) accumulation of a breakdown product (called bilirubin) of excessive destruction of red blood cells (bruises often have localized jaundice in the early stage of healing), 2) a failure of the liver to remove the normal amounts of bilirubin, or 3) failure of elimination of bilirubin via the bile that is normally made in the liver and dumped into the intestine as a waste product.

After listening to me, Conrado affirmed:

"Yes, it is a case of complex jaundice. It has caused by a terrible fit of anger that our friend threw at home. Allowing herself to be controlled by anger, she developed an obstinate hepatitis, which resulted in the jaundice."

"And how can she be assisted?"

Conrado, placing his hand over the forehead of the medium, sent a radiant current of energy that inspired her to move her hands over the patient, from her head down to the infirmed liver.

---

[21] N.T: jaundice - a yellowing of the skin, usually showing up in the whites of the eyes, fingernails, and other lightly pigmented parts of the body surface. There are three main causes: 1) accumulation of a breakdown product (called bilirubin) of excessive destruction of red blood cells (bruises often have localized jaundice in the early stage of healing), 2) a failure of the liver to remove the normal amounts of bilirubin, or 3) failure of elimination of bilirubin via the bile that is normally made in the liver and dumped into the intestine as a waste product.

We noticed that a luminous substance, which descended as fine threads to reach the visceral area, covered the encephalic cortex.

The woman's countenance displayed an undeniable expression of relief. She left visibly happy, promising that she would return to continue the treatment.

Hilario fixed his inquiring eyes on the mentor, who was amicably accompanying us, and asked:

"Will our sister be healed?"

"It is impossible," said Aulus in a fatherly manner. "Many organs and vessels are affected. Her healing requires time."

"Then what will be the basis of her healing?"

"Passes are a transfusion of energies that alter the cellular field. Even Science teaches us that the atom is not the indivisible component of matter, but rather prior to it there are sub-atomic principles, and behind these principles lies the thought. Everything derives from the mind in the sanctuary of Nature. If we would renew our thoughts, everything within us would be modified. In magnetic healing, the sending and receiving of spiritual resources helps the patient, so that one can help oneself. The re- energized mind is able to renew the microscopic organisms in the body and healing begins. Passes, have a decisive influence in healing when received with respect and trust."

"And can it be given at a distance?"

"Yes, as long as there is harmony between the one who administers it and the one who receives it. In such a case, several spirits collaborate to promote this type of assistance. Moreover, silent prayer is the best vehicle for healing energy."

Around us the service continued.

Aulus thought our presence might overload Conrado's concentration and that we should leave, since we had already obtained the teachings that we wanted. We said our farewells to the supervisor, and returned to the main room in order to continue our lessons.

CHAPTER 15

The Healing Mediums[22]

WE SHALL HERE GIVE BUT a glance at this variety of mediums, because this subject requires extended developments for our outline; we know, besides, that a doctor, one of our friends, proposes to treat it in a special work on intuitive the healing. We shall say only that this kind of mediumship consists principally in the gift possessed by some persons of healing by the simple touch, by look, even by the gesture, without the help of any medication. It will, doubtless, be said, that it is nothing but magnetism. It is evident the magnetic fluid here plays a great part; but when this phenomenon is carefully examined, it is easily seen that there is something more. Ordinary magnetization is a real treatment, continuous, regular, and methodical; in it, things happen very differently. Nearly all magnetizers are capable of curing, if they know how to properly undertake it; but with healing mediums the faculty is spontaneous, and some even possess it without ever having heard of magnetism. The intervention of a hidden power, which constitutes mediumship, becomes evident under certain circumstances: it is so, particularly, when it is considered that most persons, whom

---

22 An excerpt from the *"The Mediums' Book"* – Allan Kardec – Chapter 14, Items 175 and 176, translated by Emma A. Wood, 1970 – USA.

we can reasonably qualify as the healing mediums, have recourse to prayer, which is a real invocation.

Here are the answers to the following questions addressed to the spirits on this subject:

1. **Can persons endowed with magnetic power be considered as forming a variety of mediums?**
   You cannot doubt it.
2. **Yet, the medium is an intermediary between the spirits and man; but the magnetizer, drawing his strength from within himself, seems not to be intermediary of any foreign power?**
   It is an error; the magnetic power resides, doubtlessly, in the man; but it is augmented by the action of the spirits he calls to his aid. If you magnetize with a view to healing, for instance, and you invoke a good spirit who interests himself in you and your patient, he augments your strength and your will; he directs your fluid, and gives it the necessary qualities.
3. **But there are very good magnetizers who do not believe in spirits.**
   Do you think that spirits act only on those who believe in them? Those who magnetize for good purposes are seconded by good spirits. Every man who has a desire to do good undoubtedly calls them; the same as by the desire of evil, and evil intentions, he calls the evil.
4. **Would he who has the power act more efficaciously, should he believe in the intervention of spirits?**
   He would do things you would look upon as miracles. "Have some persons truly the gift of healing by the simple

touch, without employing magnetic passes? Assuredly, have you not numerous examples of it?

5. **In this case is there magnetic action, or only influence of spirits?**
Both; these persons are veritable mediums, because they act under the influence of spirits; but that is not to say they would be writing mediums, as you would understand it.

6. **Can this power be transmitted?**
The power, no; but the knowledge of the things necessary to its exercise where it is possessed. A person would not suspect that he has this power if he did not believe it has been transmitted to him.

7. **Can cures be made by prayer alone?**
Yes, sometimes, if God permits; but perhaps the good of the sick person is that he should suffer, and then you believe that your prayers are not heard.

8. **Are there some forms of prayer more efficacious for that than others?**
Superstition alone can attach a virtue to certain words, and ignorant or lying spirits alone can entertain such ideas in prescribing forms. Yet it may happen that, for persons not much enlightened, and incapable of understanding things purely spiritual, the employment of a formula helps to give them confidence; in this case it is not the form that is efficacious, but the faith that is increased by the idea attached to the use of the form.

CHAPTER 16

Magnetic Properties of Matter

MODIFICATION OF THE PROPERTIES OF MATTER

16.1 MAGNETIC CURATIVE ACTION

"...ONE PART OXYGEN AND TWO of hydrogen, both inoffensive, form water; add an atom of oxygen, and you have a corrosive liquid. Without changing the proportions, often a simple change in the method of molecular aggregation can change the properties; thus an opaque body can become transparent, and vice-versa. Since the spirit has by his sole will so powerful an action on elementary matter, it may be conceived that he cannot only form substances, but can denaturalize their properties, will have herein the effect of a reactive.

This theory gives us the solution of a fact in magnetism, well known, but hitherto unexplained – that of the changes of the properties of water by the will. The acting spirit is that of the magnetizer, most frequently assisted by a foreign spirit; he effects a transmutation by the aid of the magnetic fluid, which, as has been said, is the substance most nearly approaching cosmic matter, or the universal element. If he can effect a modification in the properties of water, he can as well produce an analogous phenomenon on the fluids of the organism, and from thence the curative effect of the magnetic action properly directed.

We know the great part played by the will in all the phenomena of magnetism; but how do we explain the material action of so subtle an agent? The will is not a being, a substance; it is not even a property of the most ethereal matter; the will is the essential attribute of the mind, that is to say, of the thinking being. By the aid of this lever he acts on elementary matter, and, by a consecutive action, he reacts on its compounds, whose intimate properties can thus be transformed.

Will is the attribute of the incarnate as well as of the wandering spirit; from thence the power of the magnetizer, a power that we know to be in proportion to the strength of the will. The incarnate spirit, being able to act on elementary matter, can then vary its properties in certain limits; here we have explained the faculty of curing by laying on of hands, a faculty possessed by some to a greater or less degree." (See *"The Spiritist Review,"* July 1859.)

16.2 Magnetized Water

Among the many fluids that are of primary necessity for humanity, water is certainly one of the most important. The human body is known to be composed of about seventy percent of water. Thus, in Spiritism it is common practice to offer a small quantity of water to the patient after receiving the pass as a complement to this process and as a means of revitalizing the physical body. This is not ordinary water, because it has been saturated with beneficial fluids originated in the spiritual world under the guidance of the Spiritual Benefactors responsible for the work of passes. This is why it is called magnetized water. This special water enables the patient to retain energies and increases the absorption potentialities of restoring fluids received during the pass. This will allow the patient to continue to receive spiritual benefits between the pass sessions. It is also very helpful for the digestive organs to receive a direct influx of spiritual fluids.

Ordinary water has the possibility of conserving spiritual fluids for indefinite periods of time without having their properties suffer any deterioration. Being of an inorganic nature this substance also plays an important part in the revitalization of the physical body and is in fact the primal vehicle of vitality and thought to act as a possible link between organic and inorganic principles.

The Spirit Emmanuel refers to the magnetized water in his book *The Consoler*[23]:

103) Regarding the treatment provided by the friendly Spirits – will the magnetized water of a sick patient have similar effect on another person?

The water can be magnetized in a general way, in order to benefit everyone; it can also be magnetized with a specific character for a specific patient, in which case it should be expended for the personal and exclusive use of that patient.

---

23 XAVIER, Francisco C., "O Consolador" (The Consoler) not yet translated into English, by the Spirit Emmanuel

104) Is there any special condition required by the friendly Spirits in order to magnetize the pure water, such as the presence of healing mediums or the gathering of various elements, etc.?

Charity cannot be subject to specific situations. The presence of healing mediums, as well as the requirement of special meetings, under no circumstance should constitute the price of benefiting the sick, as the resources of the spirit guides – within this context (sphere of action) – do not depend upon the cooperation of mediumship, when taking into consideration the matter of individual merits.

CHAPTER 17

Types of Passes

17.1 Laying on of Hands

*"Now Joshua son of Nun was filled with the spirit of wisdom because Moses had laid his hands on him. So the Israelites listened to him and did what the Lord had commanded Moses. Since then, no prophet has risen in Israel like Moses, whom the Lord knew face to face, who did all those miraculous signs and wonders the Lord sent him to do in Egypt. For no one has ever shown the mighty power or performed the awesome deeds that Moses did in the sight of
all Israel."*

Deuteronomy 34, 9:12

"Jesus reached out his hand and touched the man: I am willing, he said. Be clean! Immediately he was cured of his leprosy."

Matthew 8, 3

"Then Ananias went to the house and entered it. Placing his hand on Saul he said: Brother Saul, the Lord – Jesus, who

> *appeared to you on the road as you were coming here, has sent me so that you may see again and be filled with the holy spirit."*
>
> ACTS 9, 17

WITHOUT ANY DOUBT THE LAYING on of hands is known as being one of the most common and universal practices utilized for healing purposes, as we can observe above in the citations of the Bible.

Mr. Paul Clement Jagot tells us that from a papyrus discovered by Ebers in the ruins of Thebes, the translators managed to extract a characteristic phrase: "Place your hand over the pain so that the pain can go away."

In the *"Book of Dead"* we read: "I place the hands over you, Osiris, for your own good, to make you live." It was a common practice in the Egyptian temples that the hierophant would place his hands over the sick and attain their cure. Prosper Alpini, a historian, mentions the mysterious "medical frictions" utilized in ancient Egypt that is easily recognizable as being magnetic passes.

In Greece, the Pythagorean Doctrine demonstrates that the practice of medicine by way of the hands of the Asclepiadeans was not considered to be empirical, but rather from reasoned data.

Throughout the Middle Ages, the laying on of hands, healing breath, and other manifestations of human magnetism were practiced. As the magnetizers of the Middle Ages utilized the "physical contact" they were known as "the ones who touch." Actually, since the time of King Louis IX of France (some say since Clovis) it was a tradition among the French Kings to touch the sick in order to cure them. This practice was utilized until the time of King Henry IV.[24]

---

[24] Mr. Paul Clement Jagot, Historic Summary in the book *"Initiation to the art of healing through Human Magnetism."* Chap. 5, pages 34 to 36.

Apart from the historical references regarding the laying on of hands, we can affirm that the technical structure of this type of pass is so simple that there is not too much to be learned. The pass giver extends his arms forward in front of his body, placing his hands (separating his fingers) over the head of the patient, or any other area that requires treatment. The hands should face downward, without any muscular contraction. Apart from that, the most important point is to maintain oneself in fervent prayer, asking the Lord for His blessings for the patient. The pass giver will also utilize his will power to assist, and to transmit good positive energy, forgetting any kind of imperfection at this moment, that he still harbors within, such as pride, vanity, resentment, or any material worry he may have. This is literally a sacred moment.

It is important to remember that among the principles, a general rule exists that was introduced to us by Jesus in the Lord's Prayer: *"Thy will be done on Earth as it is in Heaven."* This means that we have to subordinate our action and our request for help and assistance to what is already determined by Divine Justice.

As a rule, the patient is under a psychic imbalance or disorder. For this reason, it is recommended to commence with a dispersive pass prior to the laying on of hands. By doing this, the pass giver will be removing and rearranging the unbalanced energies.

The laying on of hands may be performed with one hand (simple imposition) or both hands (double imposition). The most common technique is to utilize both hands. (Some examples of laying on of hands can be seen in the next page)

It is commonly utilized for the donation of fluids or to separate the obsessor or any negative spiritual influence from the patient.

Examples Of Laying On Of Hands

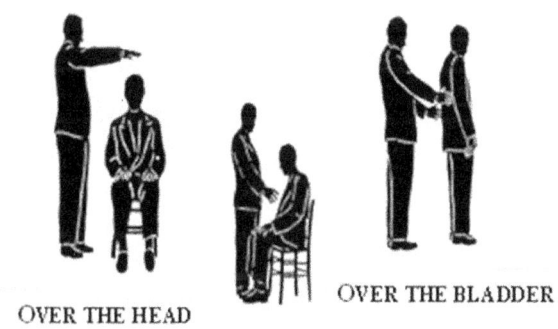

OVER THE HEAD

OVER THE SOLAR

OVER THE BLADDER

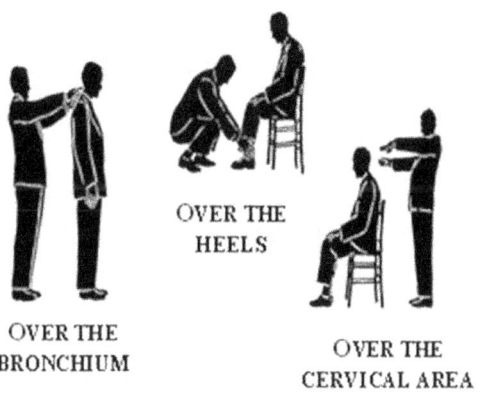

OVER THE BRONCHIUM

OVER THE HEELS

OVER THE CERVICAL AREA

17.2 Longitudinal Passes

As a technique, the longitudinal pass is the one that is given to the patient along the body, starting at the head and going downward to the toes (or to the area that needs assistance). The Pass Givers' hands should remain open with their arms outstretched, but

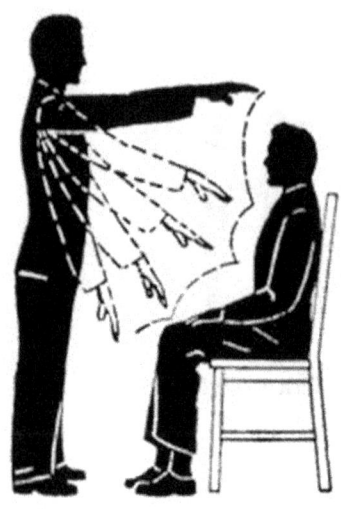

without any contraction and with the necessary flexibility required to execute the movements.

When the longitudinal pass is applied slowly (approximately 30 seconds from head to toe) and at close range to the patient's body (approximately 2 to 6 inches) it saturates the patient with energies, and achieves an active and stimulating effect.

When the longitudinal pass is applied slowly and at a distance of 6 to 40 inches, it has a tranquilizing effect on the patient.

The longitudinal pass, also known as "Great Current," when applied very rapidly (approximately 5 seconds from head to toe) and at a distance of more than 6 inches, has an exceptional dispersive power. It also has a tranquilizing effect, regulating the circulation of the blood.

Longitudinal Pass is used:

- To move and to distribute fluids
- To separate Entities from the perispirit of the patient
- In cases of somnambulism
- To aid in sleeplessness

Great Current Pass is used:

- To move, distribute and to normalize fluids
- In fevers

- In cases of anguish and affliction
- To calm the patient down

Note: A great amount of Current Pass is always applied from head to toe.

The Five Movements Of Longitudinal Pass

First: Concentrate and pray, while assuming the position to commence the Healing Process

Second: Place your hands over the top of the head (the crown center of force) and move them downward until you reach the basic chakra.

Third: Open your hands wide, in order to release the negative energies that were displaced and removed during the second movement.

Fourth: Close the hands and return them rapidly to the starting point, which is the laying on of hands, and restart the pass.

Fifth: Once the pass is finished, close your hands and keep your arms away from the body.

17.3 ROTATIONAL PASSES

This kind of pass is normally applied with the palm of the hand or with the fingers. The pass giver will slowly start with rotational movements from the right to the left, or vice-versa, on the part of the body that needs to be healed, at a distance of 4 to 6 inches. When applied with the fingers, they should be bent in the direction of the area that needs to be magnetized, without rigidity and muscular contraction. Then the pass giver starts with the concentric movements around the area for a few minutes. The rotational pass is extremely stimulating, therefore, being utilized when the intention is to treat vomiting, obstructions, abscess, irritation in the intestines, cramps, constipation and general indisposition of the lower abdomen. It also helps in cases of dehydration and malnutrition.

If necessary, the pass giver can use both hands, one that remains steady at the back of the head (the left hand for a right handed person or vice-versa) and the other that will be applying the rotational pass to the needed area.

DISPERSIVE ROTATIONAL PASS
The pass giver places his hands over the part of the body that needs to be healed at a distance of 4 to 6 inches, or a little closer. With the palm of his hands facing the area that requires a dispersive pass, he maintains his fingers totally opened and stretched as

if he wanted to fold them backwards. At this time the magnetizer will clearly perceive the concentration of energy in the center of the palm of his hands starting to leave through his fingers in the direction of the etheric space.

In this, as in all passes, let us pay attention to our mental attitude; as, it is not only the simple mechanical movements that contribute to the release of the dispersive fluids to help the patient. Our mental command is also indispensable.

17.4 Transverse Passes

After the Dispersive Rotational Pass, the Transverse Pass is the one most indicated to disperse accumulated energies. However, its usage presents some inconvenience in its utilization within the Spiritist Center. Let us see why:

1. The pass giver will stand in front of the patient at a distance of approximately 12 to 20 inches.
2. He will then extend his arms in a double imposition of the hands with his thumbs contracted and facing downward as if he were trying to hide them.
3. The pass giver will open his arms horizontally (cross position) rapidly.
4. He will return to the initial position in a rapid movement and will repeat the sequence a few times.

The use of this type of pass requires very rapid and intense movements of the hands and arms, as well as enough physical space for its performance.

The Transverse Pass can also be "crossed." The technique and purpose of this pass are the same, except that the arms will be crossed in front of the patient. Instead of having his arms extended, the pass giver places one arm over the other in an "X" shape. This technique, however, presents more difficulty than the first because it places the pass giver in the risky position of unintentionally striking the patient.

Since there are simpler forms of passes with greater capability of dispersing, we do not recommend this pass as a regular practice.

17.5 Perpendicular Passes

Like the Transverse Pass, the Perpendicular Pass is considered to be extremely dispersive. The pass giver stands at the side of the patient, starting with the laying on of hands, at the side of the head (as shown in the figure). The pass giver then simultaneously lowers his hands, one in front (right, for the right-handed person or left, for the left-handed person) and the other in the back of the patient to the feet, in a longitudinal pass. This can be repeated more than once. Its power of general dispersion is extremely efficient.

This type of pass is very often utilized for treatment of the nervous system.

CHAPTER 18

The Healing Breath

"The Lord God formed the man from the dust of the ground and breathed into his nostrils, the breath of life, and the man became a living being."

GENESIS 2: 7

"The wind blows wherever it pleases. You hear its sounds, but you cannot tell where it comes from or where it is going. So it is with everyone born of the Spirit."

JOHN 3:8

IN THE FIRST BIBLE CITATION, we find the symbolism of the human genesis, where we encounter a notable and unquestionable register of the vitality of the healing breath. In the second citation, we see Jesus in an explanation, still inaccessible to our knowledge and understanding, presenting the spiritual creation in the figure of the Divine Breath.

There are two types of Healing Breath therapies: Cold and Hot.

18.1 The Cold Healing Breath or Cold Insufflations

The Cold Healing Breath (CHB) is applied at a distance of approximately 12 inches to over 40 inches away from the patient. The further away the pass giver is from the patient, the colder it will be.

The procedure is to blow rapidly and vigorously over the area of the body that needs to be healed, as if we were blowing out a candle from a distance.

Its' effects are refreshing and tranquillizing, constituting a precious process of dispersion.

It can be used:

- To combat headaches
- For nervous breakdown
- For burns
- For convulsions caused by fever
- To separate the obsessor from the one who is obsessed
- To stop epileptic seizures

When applied in the area of the eyes and the forehead, it awakens the patient who is magnetically asleep due to the action of a magnetizer or because the patient is under the influence of an obsessor.

The technique of the cold healing breath is usually very efficient in cases of patients suddenly "taken over" during the pass, and that still remain in a lethargic state after such a procedure.

In this case, the pass giver applies cold healing breath with a greater vivacity in the area between the eyes (the frontal center of force).

Please be cautious and give the patient support during this procedure, as upon awakening he will usually feel somewhat dizzy and susceptible to falling.

18.2 The Hot Healing Breath or Hot Insufflations

The Hot Healing Breath (HHB) is a type of magnetic pass commonly used by most people to assist in alleviating pain or any kind of suffering, even in asphyxia. Even though its restoring health principles are still unknown, its beneficial action cannot be ignored. As opposed to the technique of the cold healing breath, there may be physical contact when applying this technique. In this case, a handkerchief is placed upon the area that needs the magnetization and the pass giver, after taking a deep breath, puts his mouth over the tissue and proceeds exhaling forcefully and as slow as possible, until he completely expels all the air from his lungs, without any contraction or unnecessary effort in the area of the mouth. After he has finished, he lifts his head, remove his mouth from the tissue and inhale once again through his nostrils, from a healthy source of purified air, and then he repeats the process to a maximum of six times, as this is an extremely strenuous technique.

Another way of applying this type of pass is to bring the mouth over the sick area (without making contact) and then exhaling, as if he were trying to warm his hands from the cold or to clean his eyeglasses. This procedure can also be done over the area covered by a tissue.

Because the HHB is a stirring kind of pass, it should never be utilized in cases of deep lesions, and especially in cases of aneurysm of the heart or the aorta. It should not be used in persons in an advanced stage of tuberculosis.

The Hot Healing Breath can be used:

- In cases of ingurgitation and pain
- In obstructions
- In asphyxia
- In stomach ache
- In hepatic or nephritic cramps
- In headaches
- In glandular disturbances
- In ear ache
- In deafness
- On articulations

It can also be applied over the top of the head, at the cerebellum, the forehead, the eyes, the ears, the gastric region, the spleen, the kidney, the bladder, the spine and the heart.

Nevertheless, some advice must be given to the pass giver who wishes to make use of this technique:

1. In order to be fit enough to utilize the Healing Breath, the pass giver must have balanced health, especially the

respiratory and the digestive organs, in addition to being free of any clinical condition of the heart.
2. A well-balanced nutrition should be observed, as well as care in brushing teeth, in order to avoid an offensive odor from the mouth.
3. As this technique requires a closer range between the pass giver and the patient, the pass giver must be conscientious and not allow inappropriate movements or have disrespectful thoughts toward the patient.

To conclude, it must be pointed out that due to the active and concentrated aspect of the Healing Breath, a localized dispersive pass is suggested afterwards. Therefore, a dispersive rotational pass is recommended after the Healing Breath.

18.3 THE HEALING BREATH[25]

"Speaking of which…" said Ismalia, "we mustn't delay. It's almost time."

As if he had suddenly remembered all the work he had to do, the administrator said to his partner:

"Olivia and Madalena need to be advised concerning the provisions that are urgently needed for tonight. We'll need the collaboration of a few more breath technicians. There are quite a few brothers and sisters in a serious state after having been overcome by "powerful physical sensations.""

---

[25] An excerpt from the book *"The Messengers"* chapter 19, from the spirit Andre Luiz, received through automatic writing by Francisco C. Xavier, published by EDICEI.

"Breath technicians?" I asked, perplexed, before Ismalia could make any remarks about this type of service.

"Yes, my friend," answered Alfredo. "Even on earth, the healing breath is a sublime human privilege. However, while incarnate we are very slow to lay hold of the great treasures that are ours by right. We usually live there, wasting time on fantasies, believing in futilities or feeding suspicions. Those who could grasp the far reaching implications of this subject could create highly effective breath therapy processes."

"But is such a gift available to any incarnate spirit?" asked Vicente, sharing my surprise.

Alfredo thought for a few seconds "and answered:

"As with magnetic passes, which can be done by a large number of people with noticeable benefits, the healing breath may also be used by most humans with impressive results. However, we must add that at any time and in any situation, individual effort is indispensable. Every worthwhile accomplishment requires serious support. The Divine Good demands human willingness to manifest itself actively. Our breath technicians were not trained quickly. They practiced for a long time and acquired experience at a high price. With everything, there is a right way to start. They are respected workers because of what they have achieved. They earn significant returns and enjoy enormous respect, but for all this they must "preserve the purity of their words and the holiness of their intentions."

Understanding the interest that his words were arousing, the administrator continued after a brief pause:

"In the physical realms, in order for the breath to be sufficiently established, it is imperative for the individual to have a healthy stomach, a mouth free of evil and accustomed to saying good things, and a righteous mind that is interested in helping. By complying with these requirements, we will have a calming and invigorating breath that is both stimulating and healing. By means of such breath, health, comfort and life can be transmitted on the earth's surface as well as here."

And since Vicente and I could not "hide our perplexity, Alfredo remarked:

"This is nothing new. In addition to physically touching those he healed, Jesus sometimes touched them with the divine breath. The breath of life runs through all creation. Every sacred page that comments on the beginning of life refers to it. Haven't you ever thought of the wind as the creative breath of nature? As for me, ever since I entered Campo da Paz, where I was taken in in the worst spiritual condition imaginable, I have been learning wonderful lessons on this subject, so much so that in heading this Station I have encouraged as much as possible the training of new workers in this area. I have offered special recompense to those who decide to begin this specialized task because not everyone can do it."

"Ismalia greeted some important looking workers, who were preparing for this task.

Impressed with what I had heard, I closely observed the preparations.

However, when I was alone with Aniceto once more, I shared my enormous surprise with him. He answered in a confidential tone:

"You are forgetting that the Bible itself, alluding to the creation of Adam, says that the Creator breathed on the form he had created, passing the breath of life to him. Referring to our incarnate brothers and sisters, we must realize, Andre, that even coming from imperfect but good-willed humans, every breath with the intention of relieving or healing is significant because all of us "are direct heirs of the divine power. Moreover, it is also necessary to realize that we are not dealing with something exclusive. You yourself spent a short while in our Ministry of Assistance. There is a large department there that specializes in the subject, and where worthy coworkers devote themselves to this type of work. On the physical plane, every mouth with a holy intention can render appreciable aid, but generous and pure mouths can distribute divine aid, transmitting vital fluids of health and comfort."

I was hoping that Aniceto would continue by showing me the magnetic qualities of breath, but Alfredo enthusiastically and eagerly approached us, exclaiming:

"The moment of our assistance and "prayer work has arrived!"

"It will be our pleasure to accompany you," answered Aniceto with a smile.

We had to end the lesson and attend to other duties."

BIBLIOGRAPHY

Kardec, Allan. **The Gospel According to Spiritism.** Trans: Janet A. Duncan. London: ALLAN KARDEC Publishing Ltd. 2nd Edition.

Kardec, Allan. **The Spirits' Book.** USSF - 2017 Questions 420, 658 to 666.

Kardec, Allan. **The Mediums' Book.** Trans: Anna Blackwell. Rio de Janeiro: FEB.

Kardec, Allan. **Genesis**. Spiritist Alliance for Books/Spiritist Group of New York. Chapter 14, items 2 to 6.

Duncan, Janet. **The Healing Brochure.** Prepared by Allan Kardec Study Group of London, 1993. (Cited on items 1, 4-10 of this book).

Leadbeater, C. W. **The Chakras.** Illinois: The Theosophical Society House, 1927.

Andre, Prof. Jorge. **Forças Sexuais da Alma**. Rio de Janeiro: FEB, 1987.

Zimmermann, Zalmino. **O Perispirito**. Campinas: Published by CEAK, 2000.

Denis, Leon. **Into the Unseen**. USSF: - 2nd part Chapter 15.

Xavier, Francisco C. / Emmanuel. **O Consolador**. Rio de Janeiro: FEB. Question 95.

Xavier, Francisco C. / Andre Luiz. **The Messengers**. Edicei. Chapter 19.

Xavier, Francisco C. / Andre Luiz. **In the Domain of Mediumship.** Spiritist Alliance for Books/Spiritist Group of New York. chapter 17.

Scripture taken from the HOLY BIBLE - NEW INTERNATIONAL VERSION, Copyright © 1973, 1978, 1984, by International Bible Society. Used by permission of Zondervan Publishing House. All rights reserved.

The "NIV" and "New International Version" trademarks are registered in the United States Patent and Trademark Office by International Bible Society.

www.ingramcontent.com/pod-product-compliance
Lightning Source LLC
Chambersburg PA
CBHW071707040426
42446CB00011B/1954